D1460999

teach®
yourself

mussolini's italy
david evans

For over 60 years, more than
40 million people have learnt over
750 subjects the **teach yourself**
way, with impressive results.

be where you want to be
with **teach yourself**

Every effort has been made to trace copyright for material used in this book. The authors and publishers would be happy to make arrangements with any holder of copyright whom it has not been possible to trace by the time of going to press.

For UK order enquiries: please contact Bookpoint Ltd, 130 Milton Park, Abingdon, Oxon OX14 4SB. Telephone: +44 (0) 1235 827720. Fax: +44 (0) 1235 400454. Lines are open 09.00–18.00, Monday to Saturday, with a 24-hour message answering service. Details about our titles and how to order are available at www.teachyourself.co.uk

For USA order enquiries: please contact McGraw-Hill Customer Services, PO Box 545, Blacklick, OH 43004-0545, USA. Telephone: 1-800-722-4726. Fax: 1-614-755-5645.

For Canada order enquiries: please contact McGraw-Hill Ryerson Ltd, 300 Water St, Whitby, Ontario L1N 9B6, Canada. Telephone: 905 430 5000. Fax: 905 430 5020.

Long renowned as the authoritative source for self-guided learning – with more than 40 million copies sold worldwide – the **teach yourself** series includes over 300 titles in the fields of languages, crafts, hobbies, business, computing and education.

British Library Cataloguing in Publication Data: a catalogue record for this title is available from the British Library.

Library of Congress Catalog Card Number: on file.

First published in UK 2005 by Hodder Education, 338 Euston Road, London, NW1 3BH.

First published in US 2005 by Contemporary Books, a Division of the McGraw-Hill Companies, 1 Prudential Plaza, 130 East Randolph Street, Chicago, IL 60601 USA.

This edition published 2005.

The **teach yourself** name is a registered trade mark of Hodder Headline.

Copyright © 2005 David Evans

Typeset by Transet Limited, Coventry, England.
Printed in Great Britain for Hodder Education, a division of Hodder Headline, 338 Euston Road, London NW1 3BH, by Cox & Wyman Ltd, Reading, Berkshire.

Hodder Headline's policy is to use papers that are natural, renewable and recyclable products and made from wood grown in sustainable forests. The logging and manufacturing processes are expected to conform to the environmental regulations of the country of origin.

Impression number   10 9 8 7 6 5 4 3 2 1
Year   2010 2009 2008 2007 2006 2005

contents

introduction

'*Italien ist ein geographischer Begriff.* (Italy is a geographical expression.)'
(Prince Metternich, the Austrian Chancellor in 1849.)

It is necessary to remember that although there have always been Italians, there has not always been an Italian nation. Even so, few nations can reflect upon a more flamboyant history filled with such outstanding achievements as Italy.

Today, some 1,500 years after its demise, many Italians would consider the greatest period in their history to have been that of Imperial Rome. Between the eighth century BC and the fifth century AD, the Roman Empire grew to extend from Britain in the north to Egypt in the south and from Portugal in the west to Iraq in the east. It first created and then preserved one of the greatest civilizations of the Ancient World and the Romans grew wealthy on the spoils of their conquests.

Victorious Roman legions brought with them justice and peace, *Pax Romana*, as well as a system of government, their language, Latin, a system of well-structured roads, and the often cruel entertainment provided at amphitheatres. The emblem of the Roman magistrate was an axe buried in a bundle of rods, the *fasces*. In the twentieth century this was to be adopted as a symbol by the supporters of Benito Mussolini who called themselves Fascists. As we shall see, the Italian dictator promised to recreate the glory of Ancient Rome by restoring the ruins of the Pantheon, the arch of Constantine and Vespasian's great amphitheatre, the Colosseum. Today, evidence of the quality of Roman architecture can still be seen by visitors to the remains of ill-fated Pompeii at the foot of Mount Vesuvius.

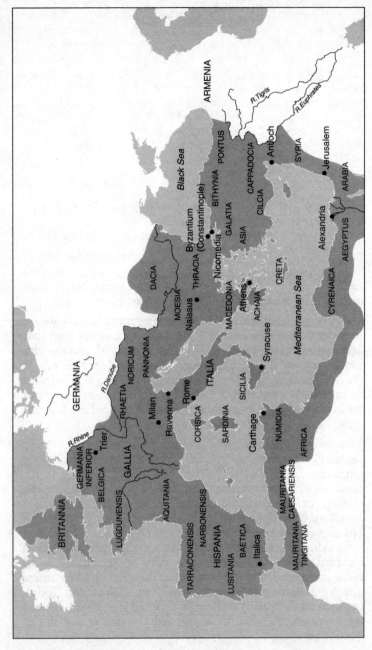

figure 1 the extent of the Roman empire

It was during the latter period of the Empire that the Christian church was first established in Rome. St Peter's authority for founding the church was based on the pronouncement of Jesus Christ, 'Thou art Peter and upon this rock I will build my church.' In AD 337, during the reign of the Emperor Constantine, Christianity became the official religion of the Roman Empire. Fifty years later, the bishop of Rome was given the title 'Pope' and was recognized as the head of the Roman Catholic Church. Successive Popes were to become not only spiritual leaders but also temporal or worldly rulers and important political figures.

The glory of Rome was not to last. In AD 410, the sacking of the city by the Goths effectively marked the end of the Roman Empire and during the centuries that followed, Italy existed as a series of independent states on the fringe of what was known as the Holy Roman Empire. By the middle of the thirteenth century many of the states had fallen under foreign domination.

In the fifteenth and sixteenth centuries, during a period known as the Renaissance, Italy saw a revival of an interest in learning and particularly Greek and Roman culture. The movement, which started in Florence, witnessed the emergence of a number of great painters and sculptors that included Leonardo da Vinci, Raphael, Michelangelo, Titian, Donatello and Masaccio.

It was Napoleon Bonaparte's victorious campaign in Italy in 1796 that first gave Italians the experience of having a national identity but after the French emperor's defeat in 1815, the country lapsed back into its former chaotic condition. In 1849, the Austrian Chancellor famously discounted Italy when he referred to the country as 'ein geographischer Begriff', 'a geographical expression'.

When it came, the heroes of the Italian struggle to unify their country, the *Risogimento*, were the republican minded patriot, Giuseppe Mazzini, the heroic adventurer, Giuseppe Garibaldi, and the Piedmontese aristocrat, Count Camillo Cavour. They had enormous difficulties to overcome – regional differences and self-interest, poor communications, and the opposition of the Austrian Habsburgs who dominated the north of the country and Pope Pius IX who sought to safeguard his interests and his lands, the Papal States – before national unity was finally achieved. During the 1850s and 1860s, it was Cavour's state of Piedmont that championed the cause of Italian unification. A major step forward came in 1859 when Cavour won the support of France for a war against Austria and, as a

figure 2 Italy at the time of the *Risogimento*

result, a number of states overthrew their autocratic regimes and united with Piedmont. Elsewhere, Garibaldi's campaigns in Sicily and the Kingdom of Naples brought unification even closer. In 1861 at a ceremony in Turin, Victor Emmanuel II, King of Piedmont, was declared the 'King of Italy'. Now only Venetia and Rome needed to be won over before national integration was complete. In 1866, Venetia was included in the new Italy as a reward for joining Prussia in a war against Austria and in 1870 Italian troops occupied Rome. This meant that struggle for Italian unification was over and the country had a true capital city. The statesman Massimo d'Azeglio indicated that his countrymen still faced a problem of identity when he commented, 'Now that we have made Italy, it is necessary for us to create Italians.'

01 the Italy into which Mussolini was born

This chapter will cover:
- Mussolini's family background
- the political, economic and social structure of Italy in the 1880s
- the relationship between the Church and the Italian State
- the years of *transformismo*
- anarchism, socialism and reasons for discontent
- the political career of Giovanni Giolitti.

'The country (Italy) is sick politically and morally, but the principal cause is that the classes in power have been spending massive sums on themselves, and have obtained the money almost entirely from the poorer classes of society.'

(Giovanni Giolitti (1842–1928)
in a speech made in 1900.)

The Mussolini family

On 29 July 1883 in a run-down house in the hamlet of Verano di Costa close to the village of Predappio, a baby son was born to Alessandro and Rosa Mussolini. He was christened Benito Andrea Amilcare – Benito after the Mexican republican leader, Benito Juarez, who had earlier led an uprising against the domination of his homeland by the Church and aristocracy. His birthplace included a room that was set aside as the village school in which his mother was a teacher. Mussolini's father, Alessandro, was the son of a poor peasant, who was a staunch left-wing republican. A blacksmith with no formal education, he had taught himself to read and write. He was regarded as a man of strong character and a strict disciplinarian who was given to heavy drinking and womanizing. His wife, Rosa, was a schoolmistress whose earnings provided most of the family income. A devout Catholic, she saw to it that her children were baptized and attended church regularly. The couple had two other children, a son, Arnaldo, born in 1885 and, three years later, a daughter, Edvige. Following his birth, there were fears that the young Benito might be dumb, but he eventually learned to speak and soon appeared to be quite a bright child.

Living on such meagre earnings meant that the Mussolini family home was very sparsely furnished and the food plain, usually black bread and soup on weekdays with a little meat on Sundays. As a local socialist councillor, Alessandro welcomed political agitators to his home and on several occasions his own political activities led to his arrest. With little time to show his children any paternal affection, he brought them up to be aware of the injustices that existed in Italian society and of the oppression that workers and their families suffered at the hands of the upper classes and the Church. There are contradictory accounts of Benito's childhood, since some claim that he remained at home studying books whilst his schoolmates enjoyed their spare time playing games. Others say that he was a malicious and difficult boy who enjoyed tearing live chickens to pieces and engaging in knife fights with other boys.

He was first sent as a boarder to a school at Faenza that was run by monks of the Franciscan order. Later in his life he recalled his bitterness at being victimized because his father was a socialist and being forced to sit at a separate table set aside for children from families who could not afford to pay the full school fees. Aged only ten, he led a revolt against the severity of the regime and the inferior quality of the food provided and was expelled. Afterwards his mother taught him at home. Eventually he transferred to a school with a more liberal regime, the Collegio Giosue Carducci at Forlimpopoli. The more easy-going discipline encouraged his delinquent behaviour and he was frequently suspended. Nevertheless, he completed six years of study and gained qualifications that allowed him to teach in elementary schools.

The problems facing a united Italy

Faced by age-old rivalries, loyalties and prejudices, a lack of adequate communications and levels of poverty and illiteracy, the new Italian state faced major economic, political and social difficulties that were not to be easily overcome. The situation was made worse by the enormous differences between the north and the south.

The more densely populated northern Italy enjoyed numerous advantages over the south. Most of the nation's raw materials, mineral resources and industries were situated in the north in regions centred around Milan, Turin and Genoa. The north also had well-developed systems of roads and railways and even those engaged in farming benefited from better soil and a more favourable climate than the south. This meant that the bulk of the aristocracy, professional middle classes and skilled artisans were concentrated in the north where they enjoyed a more sophisticated lifestyle and much higher standard of living than those in the south.

Southern Italy, referred to as the *Mezzogiorno*, was backward, underdeveloped and served by less than 100 kilometres of rail track. The word *Mezzogiorno* refers to the strength of the midday sun that eroded the topsoil and made what remained arid and too poor to cultivate. Employed on large estates, the *latifundia,* owned largely by absentee landlords, the peasants used outdated farming methods to try and make a living from their fields, olive groves and vineyards. To make matters worse, the landlords showed little concern for the condition of their labourers and families whose living standards seldom rose above subsistence level, and saw no reason to use their wealth to introduce new farming methods.

Across Italy as a whole, 77 per cent of the people were illiterate. Even so, the best educational facilities were to be found in the north, whilst the children of those in the south received virtually no formal education. Consequently nearly 90 per cent of the people were illiterate. Since the franchise was dependent on literacy and property qualifications, few in the south had the right to vote, and this meant that the peasantry had little political influence.

The rise in crime and civil disorder

It is not surprising that those living in southern Italy felt disadvantaged, and reacted to their poverty by turning to banditry and violence. During the years after 1870, there was a steep rise in corruption, violence and banditry as socialist and anarchist groups encouraged the desperately poor peasantry to take matters into their own hands in order to remedy the situation. Sometimes the military had to be sent to restore order and at one stage over 100,000 regular soldiers had to be deployed to the south to deal with the lawlessness. The island of Sicily was the scene of the greatest lawlessness and it was here that the Mafia became the most active. The Mafia, or *Cosa Nostra*, was one of numerous secret societies that existed. Of long standing, it was a network of criminals that came to dominate Sicilian life. It recruited its members, the *Mafiosi*, from all social classes, attracting men of varying backgrounds, and accumulated wealth by intimidating the peasantry. It practised extortion, ran protection rackets and, protected by a self-imposed code of silence, it became involved in revenge murders and vendettas. Gradually Mafia activities extended across the whole of Italy and were taken abroad by emigrants, particularly those who left for the United States.

Relations between the State and the Church

The Pope, the spiritual leader of the Roman Catholic Church, had once ruled an area of central Italy, the Papal States, but between 1861 and 1870 these were forcibly taken from him. In 1871, the Law of Guarantees granted him sovereignty over the area immediately around St Peter's Church in Rome, the Vatican City, as well as a country residence at Castel Gandolfo. In addition, the Pope was exempt from taxation and allowed a maintenance grant of 3 million lire annually. The Vatican was allowed to appoint representatives to other countries. It also had the right to veto any laws with spiritual content and inspect seminaries, but Catholic clergy were made subject to the laws of the Italian state.

The problem was that the Law of Guarantees was passed without consulting the Papal authorities, and the Pope, Pius IX, reacted angrily by declaring himself to be 'the prisoner of the Vatican', refusing the grant and threatening to excommunicate all those responsible for the loss of his temporal power. For the next 50 years no pope ventured outside the walls of the Vatican. Pope Pius was the declared enemy of all forms of modernism, liberalism and socialism. He stated 'It is an error to believe that the Roman Pontiff is out to reconcile himself to and agree with progress, liberalism and contemporary civilization.' To make matters even worse, Pius IX called together the First Vatican Council and there declared the dogma of papal infallibility, which stated that 'when the Pontiff speaks *ex cathedra* on matters of faith and morals he is possessed of that infallibility with which the Divine Redeemer wished his Church to be endowed.' Put simply, henceforward all the Pope's religious pronouncements were to be considered divinely inspired and had to be accepted and obeyed by all Roman Catholics. The Doctrine of Infallibility had the effect of widening yet further the breach between the Church and the State. Pius IX actively encouraged all Catholics not to co-operate with the regime and forbade them to become involved in politics by not allowing them to stand as candidates or vote at elections. As we shall see, this on-going hostility between the Church and State was to continue for the best part of the next 60 years.

Financial difficulties

Following unification, the financial affairs of all the former independent states, including the burden of their indebtedness, became the responsibility of the central government. The need to spend substantial sums of money on the army and navy, finance a programme of public works and improve the transport system led to a major shortfall between government income and expenditure, and with insufficient funds to meet their requirements, the government had no choice but to increase taxation. In 1868, a grist tax was imposed on milled corn and for many, particularly in the south, this meant a further decline in living standards. Some of those that had managed to survive at subsistence levels now faced the threat of starvation.

Now that a new Italy had been created it was necessary to bring about reforms in the former economic, political and social structure of the country and challenge old-fashioned attitudes. Sweeping away old ideas was not going to be easy since many of the country's politicians lacked the vision, dynamism and integrity demanded by the dawning of a new age in Italian history. As they had done in the past, in order to gain office, deputies were prepared to be manipulative and, in order to win favours or gain promotion, openly resorted to bribery. As a consequence, people began to lose faith in their politicians who, instead of producing measures aimed at solving the country's economic and social problems, showed a lack of principle by working solely to enhance their own fortunes and other personal interests.

The constitution and government of Italy

After unification, Italy became a constitutional monarchy with a hereditary monarch, who had the right to summon and dissolve parliament and appoint and dismiss ministers. The form of government was based on a written constitution and the right to make laws was passed to an elected assembly. The constitution also guaranteed the rights and freedoms of Italian citizens.

Sovereign
A hereditary monarch with the right to
summon and dismiss parliament and appoint
and dismiss ministers.

Parliament

**Camera dei Depitati
(Chamber of Deputies)**
To consist of deputies elected
by the people. The government
to be in the hands of a prime
minister and his cabinet.

**Senato
(Senate)**
To consist of Senators
elected for life.

the Italian constitution

The parliament consisted of two chambers, the *Camera dei Depitati*, the Chamber of Deputies, and the *Senato*, the Senate. The Chamber of Deputies was the most important since it contained the elected representatives of the people. The Chamber could hardly claim to be broad based since the franchise depended on having attained the age 25, the ownership of property and educational qualifications so that out of a population of 28 million less than half a million had the right to vote. During the period 1870–6, political parties of the centre-right – liberals and moderate socialists – dominated Italian politics. All deputies, who were unpaid, came from privileged backgrounds and so, apart from a few radicals, the working classes remained largely unrepresented. General elections tended to be farcical with few genuine contests and the majority of candidates being re-elected without opposition.

With no single party ever emerging strong enough to form a majority government, all the governments of the time were weak coalitions. During the period 1870–1916, the country had 23 different governments.

table 1 Italian prime ministers 1869–1916

1869–73	Giovanni Lanza	1898–1900	Luigi Peloux
1873–6	Marco Minghetti	1900–1	Giuseppe Saracco
1876–8	Agostino Depretis	1901–3	Giuseppe Zanardelli
1878	Benedetto Cairoli	1903–5	Giovanni Giolitti
1878–9	Agostino Depretis	1905–6	Alessandro Fortis
1879–81	Benedetto Cairoli	1906	Sidney, Barone Sonnino
1881–7	Agostino Depretis	1906–9	Giovanni Giolitti
1887–91	Francesco Crispi	1909–10	Sidney, Barone Sonnino
1891–2	Antonio Di Rudini	1910–11	Luigi Luzzatti
1893–6	Giovanni Giolitti	1911–14	Giovanni Giolitti
1893–7	Francesco Crispi	1914–16	Antonio Salandra
1897–8	Antonio Di Rudini		

With deputies more interested in supporting local or factional interests than seeking to further the interests of the nation as a whole, government was often chaotic. In their search for support, the various factional interests were prepared to use intrigue and corruption, and deputies could be only too easily bribed to switch loyalties. With little progress made towards a truly democratic form of government, a system known as *transformismo* developed which was really government made possible by contrivance and duplicity. Within the system, the few radical deputies that refused to conform were bribed and transformed into loyal supporters of the government. The master manipulator of this form of government was Agostino Depretis.

Agostini Depretis and *transformismo*

By entering into deals, agreeing compromises and manipulating deputies, Depretis was able to form and sustain coalition governments. Quite unscrupulously he provoked government crises in order to reshuffle his government and get rid of difficult ministers. He was quite prepared to become involved in conspiracies and corruption to achieve his political ends and this caused disquiet amongst the Italian people about the working of their political system. However, his various premierships did witness the passing of several significant measures. In spite of its good intentions, the Coppino Law of 1877, which aimed to provide compulsory education for all children aged between six and nine, proved impossible to enforce due to the lack of teachers and school facilities. In addition, imprisonment for debt was abolished, workers were granted the right to take part in limited industrial action and the hated grist tax imposed on the grinding of corn was removed. Even so, the price of bread continued to rise. As a step towards greater democracy, the educational requirement and the amount of property needed to qualify to vote were both reduced and the age qualification was lowered to 21. These measures increased the size of the electorate from half a million to 2 million, but this still represented only 7 per cent of the population. Depretis also took steps to reduce corruption but they gained only minimal success.

In 1878, Victor Emmanuel II died and was succeeded by his son, Umberto I. The same year also saw the passing of Pope Pius IX and the appointment of Leo XIII as Pontiff. Although the new Pope was more moderate than his predecessor and sought to restore the prestige of the papacy, he still refused to acknowledge the Kingdom of Italy and showed concern at the increasing influence of socialism in Italian politics. Over the next 25 years, his concern for the condition of the poor was to earn him the nickname 'the working men's Pope'. Meanwhile on the political front, the increasingly unpopular Depretis finally died in 1887 to be replaced by his most vociferous critic, the Sicilian-born Francesco Crispi. Once in office, Crispi's policies largely followed those of his predecessor. He granted a greater degree of self-government in local affairs, further liberalized the penal code and introduced measures intended to improve public health. His premiership also coincided with a period of economic recession.

Recession, poverty and emigration

In common with other European countries, Italian trade and industry faced increased competition from cheap overseas imports, and this had an adverse effect on the country's agriculture and textile trades. Under pressure from landowners and manufacturers, Crispi increased the level of tariffs placed on imported goods. The consequences were calamitous as foreign countries retaliated by imposing higher tariffs on goods imported from Italy and this led to a major recession. As exports of wine and agricultural products slumped, so the already meagre incomes of the peasants fell further. Those living on the breadline now faced the threat of starvation. Many desperate peasant families moved to seek employment in the towns, where they lived in slum conditions so poor that there were outbreaks of cholera. Others sought a solution to their problems by emigrating abroad. During the period 1881–90, some 992,000 Italians emigrated and during the next ten years this figure nearly doubled. The first decade of the twentieth century saw 3,615,000 Italians move abroad. Some moved to nearby France, Switzerland and Austria, but the majority emigrated to the United States. As their number rose, so they fell victims of unscrupulous travel agents and employers that exploited them as they had at home. Many tried to follow their traditional occupations and worked in domestic service or in cafés and bars; others became hairdressers, street entertainers and music teachers. Over 20,000 made their home in Britain and some from Bardi in the Ceno Valley moved to the valleys of South Wales where they ran cafés known as *Bracchis*.

There were other disastrous consequences of the recession. Companies and banks began to experience difficulties, and bankruptcies became common. The slump also produced further evidence of government corruption and sleaze and this led to a storm of protests. Crispi reacted by passing a decree that strengthened and extended his powers and assumed virtual total responsibility for domestic and foreign policy decisions. However, his reputation was damaged beyond repair and in 1891 he was forced to resign.

Years of discontent and civil unrest

During the 1880s and 1890s, Italy witnessed an increase in violence and terror. In a desperate search for a solution to their problems, many people gave their support to the views of the anarchist Mikhail Bakunin and the socialist revolutionary Karl Marx. Bakunin believed in the freedom of the individual to act outside the limits imposed by established convention and government-imposed laws. He wrote:

> Freedom, morality and the human dignity of the individual consists precisely of this; that he does good not because he is forced to, but because he freely conceives it, wants it and loves it.

Marx, on the other hand, issued the clarion call for a socialist world revolution much earlier in 1848 when he declared in *The Communist Manifesto*:

> Let the ruling classes tremble at a communist revolution. The proletarians (working classes) have nothing to lose but their chains. They have a world to win. Working men of all countries unite!

Both Bakunin and Marx believed in the need for revolution to change the economic and social systems.

Socialism was slow to develop in Italy since the leaders tended to be more theorists than firebrand revolutionaries. There were extremists like the syndicalists who would have nothing to do with democratic government and had but one aim: revolution. However, the moderate Filippo Turati spoke for the majority when he championed the cause of change without violence. In 1882, the first socialist deputy, Andrea Costa, was elected to the Italian Parliament and in 1895, the Italian Socialist Party, the *Partito Socialista Italiano*, was formed.

Nevertheless, the activities of both anarchists and socialist extremists and their use of terror increased. In Naples there was an attempt to assassinate King Umberto and his wife, Cairoli, and there were bomb outrages in Florence and Pisa. On the island of Sicily the situation got out of hand and troops had to be sent to restore order. The government reacted by banning all socialist workers' associations, but this measure was counter-productive and only increased support for their cause. Whilst industrialists and bankers urged the government to take an even stronger line, King Umberto supported a more conciliatory approach to the problems. Safe in the Vatican, Pope Leo III made no comment, but certainly approved of the measures taken against the socialists. As the country edged closer to a complete collapse of law and order, there were further riots in Romagna and Tuscany and another attempt on the King's life. However, it was in May 1898 that the most serious crisis occurred.

At this time, following a further increase in the price of bread, anti-government feeling reached boiling point and demonstrators took to the streets of Milan, the capital of Lombardy. Riots led to fierce clashes between workers and the military, who opened fire on the crowd killing 80 civilians and injuring 450 others. Once peace had been restored, the ringleaders were arrested and sentenced to lengthy terms of imprisonment. The government, now led by a general, Luigi Peloux, tried to be conciliatory but there were further outrages and this forced Peloux to take more reactionary measures against the troublemakers. For a time, he ran the country along military-style authoritarian lines, but his policies failed and in 1900 he was forced to resign.

The assassination of King Umberto

The new century opened with yet another tragedy. On 28 July 1900, Umberto arrived at the town of Monza, a short distance from Milan, where he was going to present prizes at an athletics meeting. The following morning Gaetano Bresci assassinated him. Tuscan-born Bresci had earlier emigrated to the United States where he had joined an anarchist group based in New Jersey. He returned to Italy with the intention of avenging the victims of Milan. Umberto, known as 'The Good King', had always taken an interest in the condition of the Italian people and had supported measures to increase the provision of elementary education and improve communications. He had also played a major role in making Italy the first country to abolish capital punishment. Sadly, the fact that he had personally decorated the general responsible for the massacre at Milan had played into the hands of the anti-monarchists and consequently he faced increasing hostility.

His son, Victor Emmanuel III, who was to rule Italy for the next 46 years during a period that included the First World War, Mussolini's Fascist era and the Second World War, succeeded him.

Giovanni Giolitti, master manipulator

During the period 1900–14, Giovanni Giolitti dominated Italian politics. Born in Piedmont in 1842, he had briefly served as Prime Minister in 1892 but was forced to resign over his involvement in a banking scandal. He returned in 1903 and was destined to lead his country on four more occasions and even when he was out of office, he remained very influential behind the scenes.

Even though he was as prepared to engage in bribery and corruption as his predecessors, he had a much better vision of what was needed to restore the fortunes of Italy. He aimed to reduce class differences, balance the demands of different political and social groups and draw them into the centre ground in order that they would support his liberal policies. He also sought to win the co-operation of the Pope and the Roman Catholic Church. Some historians regard his policies as a move from *transformismo* to *giolittismo*! First, he had to deal with the country's industrial and social unrest. To do this, he used the military more sparingly and appealed to all Italians to reject all forms of political extremism.

Giolitti was fortunate that his early years in office coincided with a period of economic recovery that turned into a boom. As Italy's trading figures with the rest of the world improved, so unemployment fell and industry expanded. It was during this time that the Italian car giants were founded – Fiat (then known as *Societa Aninima Fabbrica Italiana di Automobili*) in 1899, Lancia in 1906 and Alfa Romeo in 1910. In 1904, the Italian railway system was nationalized and this resulted in better public services and improved transport facilities for manufacturers and exporters. Importantly, Giolitti worked to ensure that the nation's new found prosperity was used to bring about social reform and improve the lot of the poorer classes by introducing old age pensions and health insurance. More money was made available for education and responsibility for schools transferred from local communities to provincial authorities. New legislation was passed to regulate working hours and conditions covering the employment of women and children. He also sought to improve the condition of the peasants in rural areas and modernize farming methods. Major constitutional changes followed. At long last, deputies were to be paid and the franchise extended to all men aged over 30 whether they were literate or not. This had the effect of increasing the electorate to 9 million.

However, Giolitti's reforms did not please everyone since radical socialists did not think they went far enough whilst bankers, industrialists and professional men generally thought they had gone too far. As we shall see, in 1914 disagreement over Italy's involvement in the First World War led to his resignation. A moderate on the right of Italian politics, Antonio Salandra, replaced him.

Unfortunately for the newcomer, Italy was once again edging towards recession and as unemployment increased and wage cuts were imposed, political extremists known as *barricadieri* or barricaders became increasingly active and called a general strike. As tension rose, there were demonstrations and riots that culminated in violent scenes in Ancona and Romagna where strikers were confronted by strike breakers hired by local employers. During the following days that came to be known as 'Red Week', the situation further deteriorated as shops were looted in Bologna. Rioters tried to set up a commune in Ancona, and Romagna went as far as to declare itself an independent republic. With more than 100,000 soldiers needed to restore order, the strong arm tactics succeeded in forcing the workers to back down and the strike ended. There was another reason for the failure of the workers to achieve their aims – catastrophic events were happening elsewhere that were dragging Europe towards a major military conflict, the First World War.

Events in the on-going conflict between Church and State

Pope Leo XIII appeared to be more a man of the world and have a greater appreciation of the problems facing Italy and the Church than his predecessor, Pius IX. No doubt aware that Marx had referred to religion as 'the opium of the people' whilst Bakunin considered it 'collective insanity', Leo XIII both loathed and feared the advance of Godless political philosophies, after years of self imposed isolation. He once again encouraged Catholics to become involved in politics. In his encyclical *Rerum Novarum* of 1891, he had been critical of both capitalism that he said 'lay upon the toiling masses of the labouring poor a yoke little better than slavery itself' and socialism that he claimed 'wrongly worked on the poor man's envy of the rich'. Although he did not really approve of liberalism, he appreciated the need for the reforms passed by Giolitti. Lawlessness, particularly the events in Milan in 1898, grieved him greatly and he died in 1903 to be succeeded by Pius X.

... and what of Benito Mussolini during these years?

As a teenager, Mussolini enjoyed an irascible, hot-blooded and often bizarre lifestyle. He had numerous casual affairs, visited brothels and when resisted, was not above rape. With few close friends, he kept largely to himself but found time to enjoy drinking, gambling and womanizing. His teaching career was short lived and he lost his job when his violent behaviour upset the parents of children attending his school at Gualtieri.

By this time, the young Benito had started to take an interest in politics and he wrote articles for left-wing newspapers and magazines. In 1903, he moved to Switzerland. The reason for his departure is unclear but to get away from his parents to avoid military service and escape creditors have all been offered as explanations. In Switzerland, he experienced hard times, lived with down-and-outs and was only saved from dire hunger by begging and a small allowance sent by his mother. During this time, he met Angelica Balabanoff, the Communist daughter of a wealthy Ukrainian, who befriended him and encouraged him to read the works of leading political philosophers in order to develop his political views. In 1903, Mussolini was arrested as a political agitator and sent back to Italy. The following year, he spent some time in France before returning to Switzerland where he again lived in poverty. Eventually he returned to Italy where he completed his compulsory military service. The death of his mother caused him much grief born largely of the regret for the anguish he had caused her in his earlier years.

Discharged from the army, he became active in local politics, wrote for the left-wing press and made virulent attacks on Italy's ruling classes and the Roman Catholic Church. It was at this time that he met Rachele Guidi who he courted and finally married in 1915. He made quite a reputation for himself as the editor of the socialist newspaper *Avanti* (Forward) and stood as a Socialist candidate in the elections of 1913. He failed to get elected but this turned out to be the beginning and not the end of his political career.

02

Italy's imperial ambitions and search for great power status

This chapter will cover:
- the aims of Italian foreign policy
- Italian attempts to colonize parts of Africa
- the issue of *Italia Irredenta*
- alliances and treaties – Italy's relations with other European powers.

'Italy must not only be respected, she must make herself feared.'
(Victor Emanuel II (1820–78).)

Foreign policy aims

As we have seen, although united, Italy remained a backward country with limited resources and industry and hardly a candidate for great power status in Europe. However, the king, Victor Emmanuel II, saw things differently and regarded his country as being the equal of Britain, France and Germany and as having an important role to play in European affairs. The German Chancellor, Otto von Bismarck, scathingly commented that Italy had 'poor teeth for such a large appetite'.

In spite of their country's many domestic problems, Italy's leaders followed an ambitious foreign policy that had four basic aims. Firstly, there was a need to achieve parity in status and prestige with other European powers. Secondly, there was a need to settle the issue of *Italia Irredenta*. This was the name given to territories along Italy's north-east border where the people were Italian and spoke Italian but lived under Austrian rule. Thirdly, for economic reasons, industrialists and those with commercial interests supported *grandezza,* a need to secure overseas colonies. By becoming an imperial power, Italy could secure access to raw materials and lucrative overseas markets and prove herself the equal of Britain and France who both controlled vast overseas empires. Fourthly, since Italy was already overpopulated there was a need to acquire additional living space. This problem would be solved by the acquisition of colonies to which Italians could emigrate and so secure better lives for themselves and improved opportunities for their children.

table 2 the growth in the population of Italy		
National growth (millions)	**Major towns (thousands)**	
		1850 **1900**

National growth (millions)	**Major towns (thousands)**		
1852 24.4		**1850**	**1900**
1880 28.5	Rome	175	463
1911 35.4	Genoa	120	235
	Milan	242	493
	Naples	449	564
	Palermo	150	228

The issue of *Italia Irredenta*

Italia Irredenta, 'unredeemed Italy' was the name given to the regions on Italy's north-east border that, even after unification, remained under Austrian rule. These regions included the South

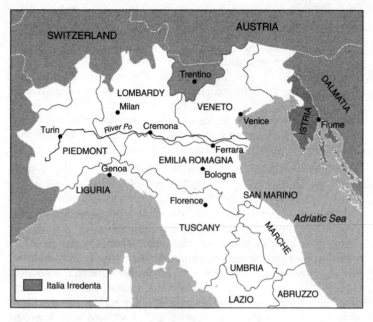

figure 3 *Italia Irredenta*

Tyrol, Trentino, Istria, Fiume, Trieste and parts of the Dalmatian coast.

These regions were largely inhabited by Italian-speaking peoples and the Trentino, whose population included 370,000 Italians, extended well into Italy. *Irredentists*, members of an Italian nationalist movement, campaigned for the annexation of these lands but their claims were ignored. As agitation increased, so there were clashes between Italian workers and Austrian officials. Even so, both countries promised to follow a policy of peace and friendship and not to engage in any armed conflict.

Italy's attempts at colonization in Africa

During that part of the middle to late nineteenth century when European powers such as Britain, France, Germany, Portugal and Belgium had carved up the continent of Africa into colonies, the so-called 'Scramble for Africa', Italy had been largely a spectator. Now, late in the day, Italy made a bid for those few territories that remained.

Italy first looked to Tunisia that was then a Turkish possession and in 1871 sent an expedition to the country with the hope of annexing it. Both Britain and France opposed the move and at the Congress of Berlin in 1878, Britain agreed that Tunisia should fall in the French field of influence in return for French agreement to their acquisition of Cyprus. The issue of Tunisia was finally put beyond doubt by the Treaty of Bardo in 1881, when the country was declared a French protectorate. Italian protests were ignored and the government showed its displeasure by joining the existing alliance between Germany and Austria-Hungary and so, in 1879, turning the Dual Alliance into a Triple Alliance (see page 20).

Italy next turned its attention to the Horn of Africa. As early as 1869, an Italian company had acquired a trading station at Assab on the Red Sea. In 1885, Italian troops occupied the port of Massawa and then advanced inland to exploit the hinterland. This led to border incidents and Italian progress was finally checked at Dogali when in 1887 Abyssinian native soldiers wiped out a force of well-equipped Italian troops. At home, the humiliation led to the removal of Prime Minister Agostino Depretis, but even worse was to come. In a dispute over rights of succession to the Abyssinian throne, the Italians made a bad choice in deciding to back Menelik and all seemed well when, in 1889, the Italians and Abyssinians agreed the Treaty of Uccialli. Afterwards, Italy claimed Abyssinia as a protectorate. However, Menelek disputed the interpretation of a clause in the treaty, claimed he had been cheated and then rejected the terms of the treaty outright. He claimed that the Italians were 'burrowing into the country like moles' and boasted that 'with God's help, I will get rid of them'. Having lost patience, an Italian army under General Oreste Baratieri used their recently acquired colony of Eritrea, as a base for the invasion of Abyssinia. On 1 March 1896, at the Battle of Adowa, the Italian army was annihilated, losing 70 per cent of its strength whilst the remnants were forced to flee in confusion. In truth, the Italian army was relatively small and badly led whilst Menelek's army of 200,000 Abyssinians was equipped with rifles earlier provided by the Italians! By the Treaty of Addis Ababa, the terms of the Treaty of Uccialli were scrapped, Italy had no choice but to accept Abyssinian independence and agreed to pay 10 million lira in reparations. The humiliation brought to an end, at least for the time being, Italy's colonial ambitions in Africa. It also ended the political career of Francesco Crispi.

By 1911, the only regions in North Africa not colonized by the great powers were Tripoli and Cyrenaica both, at least nominally, still under Turkish control. Italians had long been settling in those regions and their formal annexation by Italy had long been expected. The only opposition came from Germany almost certainly because of Italy's lukewarm membership of the Triple Alliance. An ultimatum to Turkey demanding her agreement to the Italian occupation of Tripoli and Cyrenaica was followed by a declaration of war. At home, the war was supported by the nationalist press whilst the popular Gabriele D'Annunzio used his oratory skills to stir up patriotic fervour. The Treaty of Lausanne ended the war, which had lasted a year, and, at home, the Italian victory was greeted with unrestrained euphoria. Unfortunately, there was to be a downside to the Italian success. The newly acquired territories were largely desert that offered few rewards and, to make matters worse, it placed yet another financial burden on an already flagging Italian economy.

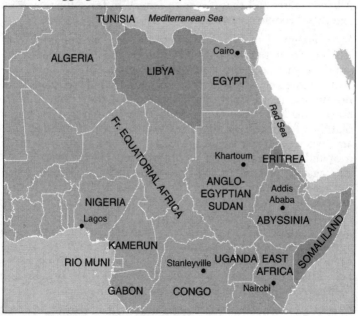

figure 4 Italy's African colonies by 1914

Alliances and treaties

One way for Italy to secure great power status was to enter into alliances and agree treaties with other major European countries. In 1879, a Dual Alliance was arranged between Germany and Austria-Hungary. Three years later, in 1882, Italy became a third member of what now became a Triple Alliance. Italy's decision to join was a reflection of her resentment of the fact that in 1881 France had established a protectorate over Tunis. Membership of the alliance also ensured Italian security since Germany and Austria-Hungary agreed to come to her assistance if France attacked her. Another advantage was that both Germany and Austria-Hungary were monarchies and membership strengthened the hand of Victor Emmanuel II in his struggle against Italian republicanism. An odd feature was that Italy now found herself an ally of Austria-Hungary, a country against which she nurtured a grievance over the issue of *Italia Irredenta*. The three countries agreed to keep the terms of the Alliance secret and that it was to remain in force for five years and then become renewable.

Membership of the Triple Alliance did not prevent Italy from seeking closer ties with Britain, France and Russia. Since the import of her coal and iron was essential to the economy, the Italian government was keen to maintain friendly relations with Britain and it was at Italy's insistence that the Triple Alliance powers made a 'Ministerial Declaration' in which they stated that their Alliance 'was not in any way directed against England' and, when the treaty was renewed in 1887 and 1890, Italy made it abundantly clear that it would not become involved in any war against Britain. In 1887, as a result of a Mediterranean Agreement, Italy, Britain and Austria-Hungary jointly undertook to maintain the status quo in the Mediterranean, Adriatic, Aegean, Black Sea and the Balkans. In a move clearly aimed at hindering any possible Russian expansion, Britain also agreed to support Italian aims in Tripoli in return for Italian support for the British in Egypt. As a gesture of their country's new found friendship, in 1907, Edward VII of Britain met Victor Emmanuel III at Gaeta on the Tyrrhenian Sea.

In spite of the rivalry over Tunisia and the fact that France had supported the papacy in its dispute between the State and the Church, Italy also sought to improve relations with France.

The Franco-Italian Convention of 1896 resulted in Italy's recognition of the French protectorate over Tunisia in return for certain political and commercial privileges. Two years later this was followed by an agreement that finally ended the damaging trade war between the two countries. Further secret agreements reached in 1900 and 1902 led to Italy and France recognizing their respective ambitions in Tripoli and Morocco. In addition, Italy promised to remain neutral in any future war that involved France. In reality, the Convention contradicted many of the undertakings taken by Italy as a member of the Triple Alliance and in 1906, when a crisis occurred over Morocco, Italy sided with Britain and France against Germany. The improved relations between the two countries was further confirmed when in 1903, Victor Emmanuel III visited Paris and the following year, President Emile Loubet of France was welcomed to Rome.

Italy also reached agreements with Russia and Austria. As a consequence of the Austrian annexation of Bosnia, by the Racconigi Agreement of 1909 Italy and Russia agreed to work together to preserve the status quo in the Balkans. The two countries also agreed not to enter into any agreement with another country without involving the other. Most important, Russia agreed to show 'benevolent neutrality' with regard to Italy's ambitions in Tripoli and Cyrenaica whilst Italy promised to support Russian plans to open the Dardanelles to her shipping. Shortly afterwards, Italy also reached an agreement with Austria-Hungary that, on the face of it, seemed to contradict her Racconigi undertakings. Again, both countries agreed not to enter into agreements with any other country without informing the other. In fairness, as the crises prior to the outbreak of the First World War deepened, Italy did do her best to restrain Austria-Hungary's warlike intentions but without success. The coming of war was soon to present the Italian government with a serious choice that was to have repercussions well into the future.

03

Italy and the First World War

This chapter will cover:
- Italy's dilemma and volte-face
- Italy's readiness for war
- the opening campaigns and the nature of war on the Italian front
- disasters and the humiliation of Caporetto
- the situation on the home front
- Vittorio Veneto – Caporetto avenged
- the end of the war and its impact on Italy
- Mussolini's role in these events.

'We shall now fight our war and blood will flow from the veins of Italy. We are the last to enter the struggle but we will be among the first to find glory.'

(The Italian poet and patriot Gabriele D'Annunzio 1863–1938.)

The coming of war

The war that started in Europe in the summer of 1914 had no single cause. Historians have attributed it to the suspicion, rivalry and enmity that existed between the major European powers that caused them to divide into two camps – the Triple Alliance of 1882 that included Germany, Austria-Hungary and Italy and the Triple Entente of 1907 that embraced France, Russia and Britain. In such a tense situation, any provocative act was likely to lead to a crisis and war. The aggressive attitude of the impulsive German Kaiser, Wilhelm II, who was described as having 'the touchiness of a prima donna and the conceit of a spoilt child' made the situation worse. The twentieth century started ominously enough with an arms race between Britain and Germany as each tried to outstrip the other in the building of battleships. In the Balkans, Austria-Hungary and Russia took advantage of the impending collapse of the Turkish Empire and competed to extend their influence in that region. The situation there worsened when in 1908 Austria-Hungary annexed Bosnia and, in the unsettled situation, the Pan Slav Movement agitated for the liberation of all Slav peoples and their union under Russian control and protection. The unrest in Balkans led to two wars in 1912 and 1913. In North Africa, Franco-German rivalry over Morocco led to crises in 1905 and 1911 and in both cases the Kaiser was humiliated and forced to back down. However, it was the assassination of Franz Ferdinand, heir to the Austrian throne at Sarajevo on 23 July 1914 that finally set Europe on course for war.

The assassins were members of a Serbian secret society, the *Ujedinjenje Ili Smrt*, Union or Death and better known as the Black Hand, who had crossed into Bosnia in order to commit the murder. In a process that the historian A. J. P. Taylor has described as 'war by timetable', the European alliances came into play as members of the Triple Alliance took up arms against the Triple Entente. Backed by Germany who offered them unconditional support, a so-called 'blank cheque', on 28 July 1914, Austria-Hungary declared war on Serbia. As Russia began to mobilize her forces in order to support Serbia so Germany demanded that her preparations for war should cease. When the ultimatum brought no response, Germany declared war on Russia. Germany next demanded a promise from the French that they would remain neutral in the war and with no such guarantee forthcoming, Germany declared war on France. British involvement in the war came when German troops, having been denied free passage across the country, invaded Belgium. By the Treaty of 1839, Britain together with other European nations including Prussia and Austria, had guaranteed Belgian independence. The Germans ignored a British ultimatum to withdraw from Belgium and consequently on 4 August 1914, Britain declared war on Germany. The irony was that the peoples of the nations involved in the war were led to believe that the conflict would be short and victory easily won. For them, the realities of trench warfare soon brought disillusionment.

Italy's dilemma

Italy had played little part in the events leading to the outbreak of war, but now decisions had to be made. Many Italians had believed that the difficulties between Serbia and Austria-Hungary would be easily settled without recourse to an armed conflict. A leading Italian socialist, Claudio Treves, expressed the view that there would be no war since it would be against the interests of the capitalist classes and the fear of revolution would force their leaders to reach a settlement. More sensibly, a former Prime Minister, Luigi Luzzatti, stated that war had to be avoided since it would lead to 'the destruction of lives, wealth, culture, civilisation…and would debase and debilitate Europe'. Even Giolitti, still amongst the most influential of Italian politicians refused to believe that 'Europe would fall prey to the folly of war'. Once these predictions proved false, Italy had to consider two important issues – whether or not to enter the war and, if they entered, on whose side should they fight, the Triple Alliance, now known as the Central Powers, or the Triple Entente, now known as the Allies.

There were those who thought that Italy should fulfil its obligations to the Triple Alliance and General Cardona, Chief of Staff of the Italian army, went as far as to prepare for war with France. To some, memories of the Italian failure to gain Tunisia made them regard France as the real enemy and involvement in a war on the side of Germany was seen as a means of increasing the prestige of Italy. In addition, religious ties meant many Italian Catholics had sympathy for Catholic Austria. Others, whilst they had no quarrel with Germany, found it impossible to side with their arch-enemy, Austria-Hungary. These, mainly *Irredentalists*, were quick to champion the slogan 'no blood, no money, no complicity with the Habsburgs'. On the extreme left of Italian politics, the syndicalists, republicans and anarchists favoured entry into the war since it would lead to instability and create circumstances favourable to revolution and the overthrow of the monarchy. War, they hoped, would be 'the fuse, the explosion, to blow away capitalism'.

In addition to those who favoured Italy's entry into the war on one side or the other or for one reason or another, there were those including the bulk of moderate liberals and socialists, who thought that Italy should remain neutral. The former prime minister, Giovanni Giolitti, represented their view in a speech made to the Chamber of Deputies in December 1914. There he stated that the murder of Archduke Franz Ferdinand at Sarajevo did not provide grounds for the Austrian decision to attack Serbia and that he saw no reason why Italy should become involved in the war. He was loudly applauded when he concluded, 'I think it is right that in the eyes of all Europe it should appear that Italy has remained loyal to the observances of her pledges'.

A *volte-face* as Italy decides for the Allies

It was remarkable that within a few days of declaring neutrality, the Italian leaders went through a complete change of mind and in the end decided to enter the war on the side of the Entente powers. It was the Nationalists, led by Enrico Corradini, who quite suddenly began to champion the need for Italy to join the war on the side of the Allies – France, Russia and Britain. Some went as far as to suggest that in order to gain the lands of *Italia Irredenta,* Italy should wage war on Austria-Hungary alone – a purely Italian war without involving the Allies of Germany. Some saw the prospect of war as the last stage in the *Risorgimento* – it was to be a war that would finally bring together into one nation all Italian-speaking peoples. In the meantime, an approach was made to Austria-Hungary to see if they would agree to surrender these territories if Italy remained neutral. It was an offer the Austrians rejected out of hand.

The views of the Nationalists, which were widely supported in the Italian press, gradually began to win the popular support of the people. Amongst those who helped to spread such views was the editor of the newspaper, *Il Popolo d'Italiana*, Benito Mussolini, and the highly regarded poet and novelist, Gabriele D'Annunzio. University educated D'Annunzio had first been elected to the Chamber of Deputies in 1887. Ever in debt, his lifestyle punctuated as it was by his many love affairs and tempestuous relationships, earned him a certain notoriety. His books, erotic and salacious as they were, proved popular and some were banned by the Roman Catholic Church. After spending some years in France, he returned to Italy in 1914 and was amongst the foremost of those who used his influence to campaign for Italy's entry into the war on the side of the Allies. As we shall see, D'Annunzio was to play a critical role in Italian politics during the war and the immediate post-war years.

Before Italy entered the war, she was in a position to drive a hard bargain and had to be tempted by secretly negotiated terms that were to form the basis of the *Patto di Londra*, the Treaty of London of 1915. These terms included the promise that she would immediately receive the active support of the British and French fleets and, after the war, gain from Austria the lands that were part of *Italia Irredenta* as well as a loan from Britain of at least £50,000,000. Clearly to merit such rewards, Italy would be expected to make a major contribution to the war. Although there were many who still opposed entry into the war and there were anti-war demonstrations by peasants and workers, the Nationalists and militarists, backed by the war mongering of Mussolini and D'Annunzio, were able to win over public opinion. On 23 May 1915, the Prime Minister, Antonio Salandra, announced that Italy was not to join the Central Powers. In his speech to the nation, he said:

> I address myself to Italy and the civilised world in order to show not by violent words but by exact facts and documents, how the fury of our enemies has vainly attempted to diminish the high moral and political dignity of the cause which our arms will make prevail...The truth is that Austria and Germany believed that until the last days they had to deal with an Italy, weak, blistering, but not capable...enforcing by arms her good right...In the blaze thus kindled internal discussions melted away and the whole nation was joined in a wonderful moral union, which will prove our greatest source of strength in the severe struggle that faces us...

Although Italy declared war on Austria-Hungary the following day, she did not enter the war against Germany until mid-way through 1916. Behind the scenes and unknown to the Italians, General Conrad von Hotzendorff, Austria's Chief of General Staff, had for some time been urging his Emperor, Franz Josef, to agree to a pre-emptive attack against Italy in order to dissuade her from joining the Allies. To his credit, the Emperor would not agree and insisted that Italy's neutrality had to be respected.

How prepared was Italy for war?

With the formal declaration of war, General Cadorna mobilized the Italian army and it was quite quickly deployed along the country's common frontiers with Austria-Hungary. During the immediate pre-war years, military expenditure had not been a priority of Eduardo Daneo, the Italian Finance Minister and he had refused the demand for £24 million by War Minister, Vittorio Zapelli, to prepare the army for war. Instead he allocated only a third of that sum.

The humiliation at Adowa in 1896 and the uninspired campaign against Turkey in 1911 had already cruelly exposed the shortcomings of the Italian army. It was clear that volunteers that joined the army were generally of poor quality and it was evident that their morale was low and that they were lacking resolve and fighting spirit. They were also badly led by inept and unimaginative generals. To what extent, if any, had the situation improved by 1915? The coming of war meant that the volunteers were now joined by largely unwilling conscripts – poorly educated peasants from the countryside and militant workers from the industrial regions. Industrial workers involved in the manufacture of munitions were exempt from military service and were considered by the soldiers to be malingerers and dodgers. Soldiers received low pay – half a lira a day – and inadequate rations. Poorly trained, they were now sent to face the harsh demands of trench warfare in a winter campaign fought in the inhospitable Alps where many were to suffer not only from frostbite but also cholera and typhus. How would they fare under the leadership of General Cadorna, a man who only a few months earlier had wanted them mobilized to fight against France? Equally important, were the Italian people ready to face the demands and sacrifices that the war would demand of them on the home front?

table 3 resources of Italy and Austria – a comparison		
	Italy	**Austria-Hungary**
Population	35m	50m
Men under arms in 1915	75,000	81,000
Divisions at the front	35	25
Fleet – all vessels	48	34
Merchant fleet	1.75m tonnes	1m tonnes
Aircraft	58	120
Military expenditure 1913–14	£10m	£22m

Italy at war

The common frontier between Italy and Austria-Hungary extended from the Swiss-Italian border to the Gulf of Venice, a distance of some 650 kilometres and for most of this distance it ran along the Alps. The Austrians, who had anticipated Italy's entry into the war, had already strongly fortified their side of the frontier so that it was virtually impregnable. To the east, the frontier roughly followed the course of the River Isonzo to the point where it joins the Adriatic Sea and although the terrain is crossed by numerous rivers and valleys, here the Alpine slopes are more gentle. Unfortunately for the Italians, the Austrians commanded all the high ground and therefore any offensive they launched would have to be fought uphill. At the start of the campaign, General Cadorna, with 35 divisions at his disposal, outnumbered the Austrians. The Austrians on the other hand had the advantage of high ground and far superior artillery. The Italian general appreciated that the area most suitable for military operations was along the River Isonzo and it was there that he decided to concentrate his main effort. Although on the face of it this was the easiest option, the river was liable to flooding and during the years 1915–18, the rainfall was exceptionally heavy. During the next two and a half years the Italians were to fight no less than 11 'Battles of the Isonzo', suffer horrendous casualties and losses of materials and, for all their effort, advance barely 11 kilometres.

In June 1915 at the start of the war and in what was to be the first of the Isonzo battles, Cadorna boldly launched a full scale offensive along the whole front line and made substantial territorial gains including the capture of Trieste. However, when the offensive was renewed in October, the Austrians were far better prepared and were able to take advantage of their enemy's shortage of shells. There were three more Battles of the Isonzo before the end of 1915 and five more in 1916 but these made few gains and the Italian armies suffered heavy casualties. Conditions along the Isonzo were appalling and when the river flooded, bridges were swept away and the system of trenches was turned into a morass of clinging mud. If anything, the suffering of soldiers in forward positions higher in the Alps was even worse since here the men suffered from the extreme temperatures and shortages of both supplies and ammunition. The shortage of munitions could in part be attributed to strikes and acts of industrial espionage on the home front as left wing militants tried to force their country's withdrawal from the war.

The entry of the United States into the war in April 1917 boosted the morale of the Allies generally but the withdrawal of Russia from the war released large numbers of German and Austrian troops for deployment elsewhere. Then in October came an Austrian offensive that was to end in the humiliation of the Italian armies – the Battle of Caporetto.

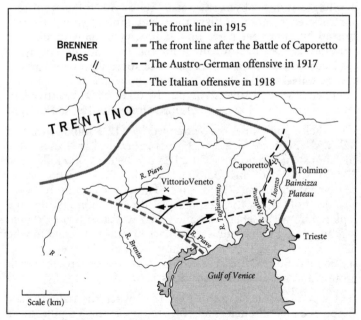

figure 5 the Italian front, 1915–18

The Battle of Caporetto

During mid-September 1917, the eleventh Battle of the Isonzo
came to an end, having brought no great success to either side.
However, the Austrians feared that they might be incapable of
withstanding another attack and decided to call upon the
assistance of their German allies. The Germans agreed and sent
seven divisions to the front and placed General Otto von Bulow
in command of both Austrian and German armies. In October,
following an artillery and gas barrage, they attacked the Italian
positions. Unprepared and demoralized, the Italians
disintegrated and retreated so that the Germans were able to
advance 22.5 kilometres on the first day of the offensive alone.
A desperate Cadorna ordered a retreat to the River Tagliamento
but again the Italians could not hold their positions and were
forced to withdraw further to River Piave.

The historian C. R. M. F. Cruttwell gives some idea of the chaos:

> Having broken contact with the enemy, they (the Italian
> soldiers) were in no hurry; they stopped to eat, drink and
> pillage. One observer notes their air of tranquil
> indifference, another that they had thrown away their
> arms but kept their gas masks; nearly as many civilians
> were fleeing more wildly from the face of the enemy,
> blocking what remained of the road space with their carts
> and household goods.
>
> (*The History of the Great War* by C. R. M. F. Cruttwell,
> Oxford University Press, 1955.)

With their supply lines over-extended by 112.5 kilometres, von
Bulow's'armies could advance no further. Italian losses were
enormous with some 300,000 taken prisoner, 10,000 killed and
30,000 wounded. In addition, they lost vast quantities of
equipment including 2,500 guns. The government's response
was to hold Cadorna responsible for the humiliation and
replace him with General Amando Diaz whilst Vittorio Orlando
was appointed Prime Minister in place of Antonio Salandra who
had resigned. The Italian army, now bolstered by the arrival of
six French and five British divisions, was now able to hold their
ground and stabilize their positions.

A change of fortune came in June 1918 when the Italians, now
supported by French and British divisions, repulsed an
attempted Austrian offensive along the River Piave. No longer
supported by German units, the Austrians faced increasing
difficulties and in October, it was Diaz's turn to launch an
offensive at Vittorio Veneto. The Austrians proved no match for

the Allies and, as their resistance crumbled, so they were forced into a retreat that in the end became a rout. At Vittorio Veneto, the humiliation of Caporetto was avenged as 300,000 prisoners were taken and 5,000 guns captured. The battle marked the final collapse of the Austrian armies on the Italian front and on 2 December, an armistice was signed at Padua.

The war at sea and in the air

Although they played less significant roles, the Italian sea and air forces were considerably more successful than their ground forces. The first sea operations came in 1915 when the Italian navy successfully rescued and ferried 260,000 Serbian soldiers and refugees across the Adriatic Sea. However, German submarines did manage to sink several Italian warships and, even worse, two battleships, the *Benedetto Brin* and *Leonardo da Vinci*, were destroyed at their home bases as a result of acts of sabotage carried out by left-wing agitators. Although the Italian navy was not involved in any major sea battles, it did carry out numerous hit and run actions against Austrian shipping in the Adriatic.

At the outbreak of war, the limited Italian air force, the *Corpo Aeronautico Militaire* that consisted of only 58 aircraft and 91 pilots was equipped with out-dated French fighter aircraft. Even so, their inexperienced pilots won numerous successes against the Austrians. Their leading ace, Francesco Baracca, was responsible for the destruction of 34 enemy aircraft. By the end of the war, Italian designers had produced the *Caproni CA* and the *Pomilio PE*, highly regarded heavy bomber and fighter aircraft. The latter played an important role in the victory over the Austrians at Vittorio Veneto.

The Italian home front

As we have seen, at the start of the war there was considerable opposition to Italian involvement in the conflict and during the war there were those who campaigned for it to be brought to an end. Whilst it might be claimed that the bulk of Italians knew little about what they were fighting for, some militants went as far as to actively engage in strikes and acts of espionage against the armed forces. To cope with this hostility, it became necessary for the government to take emergency powers and become more authoritarian. The press was gagged to prevent the spread of rumour and news that might encourage defeatism. In reality,

Italy became a near totalitarian state run by the government, military leaders and industrialists.

In 1915, the country was economically unprepared for war and the switch from peacetime to wartime production placed a heavy strain on Italian industry. Working hours were increased so that some involved in the armaments industry were expected to work up to 75 hours a week and in order to boost the size of the labour force, women were employed in increasing numbers. The demands of war meant that industry had to be mobilized and this led to centralization as large companies and banks took over sections of the country's economy. The steps taken were largely successful and some industrial units more than doubled their output. Government spending on the war led to vast profits being made and an increase in the price of goods but since jobs were plentiful and wages high, this had little immediate effect on factory workers. Even so, for scarce and luxury goods a black market developed and this allowed profiteers to make good livings. As you can imagine, soldiers home on leave from the front became aware of this and it added to their already considerable sense of grievance. Naturally, during the course of the war the morale of the Italian people varied according to their success on the battlefield. Since there were no victories to celebrate, morale was particularly low during late 1916 and 1917 and war-weariness and disenchantment set in. Such were the demands of the War Minister that, during the course of the war, the position was held by five different people. A reasonably successful enemy blockade led to food shortages, rationing and, in the end, food riots in Turin. As we have seen, left-wing extremists and pacifists further damaged the war effort by persisting with their anti-war stance and were prepared to act against the country's interests by organizing strikes and actively engaging in acts of sabotage. During 1917, they took advantage of the Bolshevik revolution in Russia to campaign even more energetically under the slogan, 'Not a man in the trenches next winter'. At one stage Pope Benedictus XV urged the Catholic Church to support the idea of a 'white peace' – a peace with no territorial gains. Although the Italian people were further disheartened by the disaster of Caporetto, the new Prime Minister, Vittorio Orlando, went some way towards re-invigorating the nation when in his first speech, he declared 'the situation will not be discussed, it will be faced'. However, it was the change of fortune brought by the victory at Vittorio Veneto that finally caused defeatism to disappear and brought the restoration of national morale.

The balance sheet of war

During the course of the war, Italy mobilized 5,230,000 men that represented 14.4 per cent of her total population. The aftermath of war left her with 650,000 dead, 947,000 wounded and some 600,000 missing. Of those mobilized, just over 39 per cent became casualties. The north-east corner of the country close to the Austrian border was ravaged whilst at sea, she also lost 650,000 tonnes of her merchant shipping. Substantial loans from her allies – including £459 million from Great Britain and £353 million from the United States – allowed her to cope with the costs of the war without imposing major tax increases on her people. Even so, her gold reserves fell by £19 million and her national debt rose from 16 billion lire in 1914 to 85 billion lire in 1919. Denis Mack Smith has estimated the final figure of the cost of the war:

> The final figure of the cost of the whole war had been 148 billion lire, that is to say twice the sum of all government expenditure between 1861 and 1913…in return Italy obtained little joy and much grief. A great deal of idealism had gone into the war on Italy's part, and much elevated patriotism, but one need not look many years beyond 1918 to see that it had been one of the great disasters of her history.
>
> (From *Italy, A Modern History* by Denis Mack Smith, Weidenfeld, 1969.)

The historian Philip Morgan summed up the divisive impact of the war:

> Italy's involvement in the First World War was the first great collective and national experience for literally millions of Italians, especially the largely peasant, conscript army. But, partly because of the imperfect nation formed since unification, and partly because of the way Italy entered the war in 1915 and the way the war was conducted, the war did not bring about national integration and unity. There was no…temporary national and political truce. Italy's wartime experience was extremely divisive.
>
> (From: *Italian Fascism 1919–45* by Philip Morgan, St Martin's Press, New York, 1995.)

With the war over and as the euphoria faded, so Italians waited anxiously to discover if the post-war conferences would honour the territorial gains promised by the Treaty of London in 1915.

Mussolini's part in the war

You will remember that when we last considered Benito
Mussolini he had gained himself quite a reputation as the editor
of a socialist newspaper, *Avanti*, but in 1913 had failed in his
attempt to get elected to the Italian Chamber of Deputies. When
a European war broke out in 1914, Mussolini took the socialist
view that it was a capitalist war in which Italy should not
become involved. As the war progressed, so he radically
changed his views and started to use his newspaper, *Il Popolo
d'Italia* to encourage Italian entry into the war. Together with
Gabrielle D'Annunzio and Riccotto Garibaldi, son of the great
patriot, he became a leading figure in a campaign that supported
Italian involvement. He even went as far as to encourage young
men to form groups and demonstrate in the streets, the groups
were called *Fasci di Combattimento*. The Socialists, who felt
betrayed by his change of heart, expelled him from the party. In
August 1915, he joined the army and, serving in prestigious
Bersaglieri Regiment, saw action in the trenches on the Italian
front. Promoted first to corporal and then sergeant, in 1917 he
was badly wounded when a grenade thrower his unit was using
accidentally misfired. After a period in hospital, he was
discharged and spent the rest of the war using his newspaper to
discourage defeatism and promote the war effort. He also used
the opportunity to put forward his own views and promote his
political career.

Mussolini had also been active in his private life. In December
1915, whilst on leave after a stay in hospital suffering from
typhus, he married Rachele Guidi in a civil ceremony. The
following year, she gave birth to a son who was appropriately
named Vittorio and in 1918 to a second son, Bruno. It is also
said that earlier, in 1915 before his marriage to Rachele,
Mussolini fathered a son by Ida Irene Dalser, the former owner
of a beauty salon in Milan. She called their son Benito Albino.
There is also evidence that Ida and Benito had, earlier in 1914,
gone through a religious marriage and he acknowledged this
and paid her alimony.

04

post-war Italy – years of crisis

This chapter will cover:
- the condition of Italy in the immediate post-war years
- the post-war settlement and the extent to which it was a 'mutilated victory'
- D'Annunzio and the issue of Fiume
- the unrest that led to *Bienno Rosso*
- the emergence of Mussolini and his Fascists.

'I have the impression that the existing regime in Italy has thrown open the succession. There is a crisis that leaps to the eyes of all…As the succession is open, we must not hesitate. We must run. If the regime is to be overthrown, it must be we who occupy its place.'

(From a speech made by Mussolini in March 1919.)

The condition of post-war Italy

During the years immediately after the war, Italy faced major economic, social and political problems. As we have seen, the war cost Italy dearly in both human and financial terms. Now, as the nation's industries struggled to revert from a wartime to a peacetime economy, so enforced wartime restrictions were abandoned and consequently during 1919 the amount of money in circulation increased to a level ten times higher than in 1914. The savings now made available meant that Italians had money to spend on all sorts of goods but sadly the economic boom that this created was short-lived, since neither industry nor agriculture had the capacity to satisfy the increased demand for their products. The consequences were shortages, price increases and rising inflation.

As elsewhere in Europe, demobilized soldiers returning home from the battlefields found it difficult to adjust to a more humdrum domestic routine. Some, because of physical injury or mental fatigue, found it impossible to settle; others were disinclined to find work and joined together with the 150,000 army deserters still at large to form marauding bands of robbers and bandits that terrorized the countryside. As far as law and order was concerned, some regions became no-go areas. Elsewhere across the country arguments raged – Why had Italy entered the war in the first place? Had it all been worthwhile? Would they now be rewarded by the territories promised in 1915?

As it was soldiers returned home uncertain of what they had been fighting for, and not very proud of the way in which they had fought. Before questions could be asked about the regiments that broke and ran at Caporetto, Italians began to brag about the land they had won for Italy. All over Italy, men opened litres of wine for the toast to victory. As the evenings grew colder, so the arguments in the cafés grew warmer and, as time went on, tinged with bitterness. Why had Italy entered the conflict in 1915? The simple answer is that she wanted land. The returned soldiers and the café politicians all agreed that this was so.

(From *Mussolini and Italy* by C. Bayne-Jardine, Longmans, 1966.)

The old pre-war problems of poverty and the north–south divide soon reappeared and recovery was hindered by shortages of coal and essential raw materials. Many of the Italian people who were poverty stricken and hungry soon became disillusioned and, as we shall see, to this was about to be added humiliation by the terms of the post-war peace settlement. Increasingly dissatisfied by the political situation, many sought a solution to their problems by turning to the parties of the Left – the Socialists and Communists. As discontent increased, so there were protest marches, demonstrations and strikes, many of which became increasingly violent.

The post-war peace settlement

In January 1919, delegates assembled in various chateaux around Paris to attend the various peace conferences being held to consider the treaties to be made with the defeated countries. The most famous of these was, of course, the Treaty of Versailles that dealt with Germany. However, the treaty that was of greatest interest to Italy was the one that considered the fate of Austria, the Treaty of St Germain. The Italian delegates to the conference were the Prime Minister, Vittorio Orlando, and his Foreign Secretary, Sidney Sonnino.

At the start, there was an immediate problem since Italian claims against Austria were based on the Treaty of London agreed with Britain and France in 1915 whilst it was now widely accepted that the terms of the peace treaties would be based on the ideas put forward by the American President, Woodrow Wilson – the 'Fourteen Points'. The Treaty of London was a secret agreement and, in spite of numerous opportunities to do so, Italy's allies had failed to inform Wilson of its terms. The difficulty was that the Treaty of London was only an ad hoc arrangement between three countries whilst Wilson's principles had subsequently been widely accepted as the basis for the peace settlement. As far as the Fourteen Points were concerned, there were three that concerned Italy. The first point stated that all diplomacy had to be conducted openly and that there were to be no more secret negotiations. The Treaty of London had been secretly negotiated. The ninth point stated that the Italian frontiers were to be adjusted along clearly recognized lines of nationality and Italians wondered to what extent these lines of nationality coincided with territorial gains promised to Italy in 1915. According to Wilson's tenth point the various peoples of

Austria-Hungary were to be allowed to develop as individual nations. Again, would this in any way clash with the terms of the earlier Treaty of London? At St Germain, Orlando and Sonnino argued that the original claims agreed in 1915 should be settled in full and when no compromise was reached and the talks broke down, both men walked out of the conference. This achieved nothing and when the treaty was finally signed on 10 September 1919, those who had been responsible for bringing Italy into the war were outraged and Italian public opinion turned against France and Britain. Just how far did the contents of the Treaty of St Germain differ from those based on the Treaty of London?

As agreed in London, the Trentino and South Tyrol passed to Italy in spite of the fact that the population of the South Tyrol included 200,000 German-speaking Austrians. Trieste was also allocated to Italy as was Istria but not the port of Fiume. This was soon to lead to an international crisis (see page 39). The Dalmatian Coast did not become a part of Italy but instead passed to the new Yugoslavia and Italy did not receive a share of Turkey. No allocation was made to Italy of any of Germany's colonies in Africa and instead they became mandates of Britain, France and South Africa. As minor considerations, Italy was allowed to extend her Libyan territories and Britain allowed her a small part of Somaliland.

Did Italy have good grounds to feel let down by her former wartime allies? Gabriele D'Annunzio, who felt that Italy had been betrayed and received scant reward for her efforts during the war, famously described the outcome as a 'mutilated victory'. The truth was that to allow some of the territories promised to Italy to go ahead would have infringed Woodrow Wilson's view that self-determination was to be the guiding principle in deciding new international frontiers. There were also other considerations to bear in mind. During the war, France and Britain had made considerably greater sacrifices than Italy and since in 1917 they had been forced to send troops to bolster the Italian armies, some may have considered that Italy had been a liability. Consequently, where Italy was concerned, they were in no mood to be magnanimous. It was also true that at St Germain, Orlando, who was normally a most articulate man, had failed to press his case with sufficient vigour. He simply did not possess the obstinacy of the French Prime Minister, Georges Clemenceau, or the guile of the British Prime Minister, David Lloyd George.

The crisis over Fiume

Of all the terms of the Treaty of St Germain, now generally regarded by Italians as 'a mutilated treaty', that caused most offence was their failure to gain Fiume. Refer to the map on page 17 and you will see that Fiume is a seaport on the River Rijecina at the head of the Adriatic Sea. Now called Rijeka, it lies in modern day Croatia. The strategic importance of Fiume was that it was one of the largest ports on the Adriatic Sea and lay at the southern terminus of a railway that led inland to Vienna and Budapest. The strange aspect of the Italian disquiet over Fiume was that, although it had a sizable Italian population, it was not amongst the territories originally claimed in 1915! A gifted orator and rabble-rouser, D'Annunzio declared 'Fiume and Dalmatia belong to Italy by divine right as well as human law'. It was his view that if Italy failed to secure Fiume then the sacrifices made during the war would not have been worthwhile.

Immediately after the war, French, British and American forces occupied Fiume. The arrival of Italian troops and the raising of the Italian flag over the port led to tension and there were incidents during which a number of French soldiers were killed and wounded. To ease the situation, a commission sent to Fiume decided that the port should be put under international control but this only succeeded in worsening the situation.

In September 1919, D'Annunzio, the 'eccentric one-eyed poet and popular hero' took matters into his own hands when he led a force of some 2,000 so-called legionaries into Fiume and occupied the port. His force consisted of a mixed bag of ex-servicemen, self-styled patriots, students, adventurers and a fair sprinkling of rogues. On his way, they raided a military depot and seized supplies and military vehicles and on their arrival were confronted by General Luigi Pittaluga, the commander of the Italian troops stationed in the city. Showing typical bravado, D'Annunzio challenged the General to shoot him first before turning his guns on his brother Italians. After some hesitation, Pittaluga backed down and with a shout of '*Viva Fiume Italiana*' he welcomed him into the city. Elsewhere in Italy, the authorities took no action against him, whilst Italians living in Fiume welcomed him as a liberator. It is claimed that Benito Mussolini, editor of *Il Popolo d'Italia*, used his newspaper to raise over 3 million lire for the insurgents but then used the money to supplement the funds of his own political party!

Taking the title 'Regent of Fiume', D'Annunzio ruled the city for more than a year. He proclaimed a constitution, set up his own militia, set up a newspaper and even printed Fiume's own postage stamps.

figure 6 a Fiume postage stamp emphasizes the region's new-found independence
© Moro Roma

In the introduction to the new constitution, D'Annunzio wrote:

> The people of the free city of Fiume, ever mindful of its Latin fate and ever intent on realising its legitimate wishes, has decided to renew its governing principles in the spirit of its new life…offering them for fraternal election by those Adriatic communities that desire to put an end to all delay, to shake off oppressive subjugation, and rise up and be resurrected in the name of the new Italy.

D'Annunzio even went as far as to order the people to remove the heads on the eagles of the civic coat of arms since they represented the Austrian and not the Roman eagle. Men serving in his militia had to wear black uniforms, give the raised arm Roman salute, later to gain prominence in Hitler's Nazi Germany, and humiliate their opponents by forcing them to drink large quantities of castor oil. As we shall see, most of these measures were later to be used by Mussolini's Fascists. He also skilfully used propaganda and arranged parades and rallies and issued emotive proclamations. From the safety of Fiume, D'Annunzio shouted defiance and abuse at Italy's former wartime allies and poured scorn on Italy's Prime Minister, Francesco Nitti, by referring to him as a worthless coward.

Some historians are of the view that his real motive was to overthrow the Italian government and establish his own dictatorship. In spite of the insults, Nitti began to exert pressure on him to withdraw from Fiume and when, in June 1920, Giolitti returned as Prime Minister, he went over the head of D'Annunzio and negotiated a settlement with Yugoslavia over the future of Fiume.

The Treaty of Rapallo, 1920

In November 1920, at Rapallo, a town south of Genoa and on the Ligurian Sea, Italian and Yugoslav delegates met to try and settle the issue of Fiume. Foreign Minister, Carlo Sforza and War Minister, Pietro Badoglio represented Italy and although Giolitti did not take part in the discussions, he arrived later to sign the final agreement. By the terms of the agreement, Italy was to occupy the whole of Istria, Zara and a number of islands in the Adriatic whilst the remaining islands and Dalmatia were to remain part of Yugoslavia. Fiume, the cause of all the problems, was to become an international city under international control. The treaty led to much improved relations between Italy and Yugoslavia and allowed both countries to collaborate and develop trading opportunities in the Balkans. Do not confuse this Treaty of Rapallo with another treaty of the same name signed a few months later, in April 1920, between the Soviet Union and Germany.

It would seem that the Treaty of Rapallo rendered D'Annunzio's continued occupation of Fiume pointless but he did not see it that way. Instead of accepting the terms and retiring from the port gracefully, he declared war on Italy! The Italian government ordered the blockade of the port and this led to clashes between D'Annunzio's supporters and the Italian army. Finally, the battleship *Andria Doria* was sent to bombard Fiume into submission. Although D'Annunzio defiantly swore to die in Fiume rather than surrender, on 5 January 1921, after 15 months in occupation, he led his legionaries out of the city and the Italian army took command. On the one hand, the Fiume incident may be regarded as ridiculous with D'Annunzio in the title role of a comic opera, on the other there were aspects of the affair that suggested ill for the future. Remember that the use of military aggression used to achieve political ends had been received with popular acclaim. Again, was it possible that D'Annunzio's aim was to pre-empt Mussolini so that he became the future Fascist dictator of Italy? At that time, he was certainly

more popular than Mussolini but after his withdrawal from
Fiume his prestige began to decline though he still remained a
serious rival and contender for power.

Mounting political problems

To many, the Italian government had proved itself weak in
failing to obtain the territories promised in 1915 and opposing
D'Annunzio's actions with sufficient vigour. However, these
were not the only problems that faced the country. Italy
remained a poor country with large numbers of the peasantry
and industrial workers living in dire poverty. Inflation had led
to significant price rises that had not been matched by wage
increases and the value of the lira had fallen to just 20 per cent
of its pre-war level. Unemployment, already worsened by the
return of demobilized soldiers, was worsened by the fact that
the United States had passed an immigration law that restricted
the entry of Italian emigrants. With industry and agriculture
slow to recover from the war, exports virtually at a standstill
and burdened with massive war debts, the Italian government
seemed to be totally inadequate in finding answers to her
mounting economic problems. In such circumstances, desperate
peasants and workers became increasingly militant and engaged
in strikes, demonstrations and riots. As political opinions
polarized, many were of the opinion that a solution might be
found by following the example set by the success revolution
brought about by Lenin's Bolsheviks in Russia. Others looked to
the extreme right for salvation and thought the answer lay in
policies now being advocated by Mussolini. *Transformismo* had
disappeared as political parties were no longer inclined to form
coalitions but instead have their own political identity.

No longer able to cope with the chaos and disruption, Orlando's
government fell in June 1919 and in the elections that followed,
the Socialist PSI (*Partito Socialista Italiano*) won nearly 40 per
cent of the votes and was by far the largest party represented in
the Chamber of Deputies.

Campaigning for a programme of social reform, the Christian
Democrats (the *Partito Democrazia Cristiana*) came second
with 20 per cent of the votes. The former ruling parties, the
Liberals and Conservatives, both lost heavily.

Mussolini's bandwagon begins to roll

At the end of the war, Benito Mussolini was still really only an ex-soldier turned embittered journalist with a hatred of his former political party, the Socialists. It was on 23 March 1919, in a hall in the Piazza San Sepulcro in Milan, he took the first steps towards forming a new political party. In a lengthy speech to a handful of supporters that included war veterans and disgruntled Socialists, he said:

> The official Socialists want to give Italy an...imitation of the Russian experience. This all socialist thinkers are opposed to because Bolshevism, far from abolishing classes, entails a ferocious dictatorship. We are strongly opposed to all forms of dictatorship, whether of the sword or the cocked hat, of wealth or of numbers. The only dictatorship we do acknowledge is that of will and intelligence. We should quickly succeed in creating a number of *Fasci di Combattimento*, then we shall co-ordinate their activities in all centres of Italy.

In 1919, the future of Mussolini's new political party, the *Partito Nazionale Fascista*, seemed bleak. In that year, he fought the general election on policies that still seemed extremely left wing. He supported the abolition of the right of people to own private property and promised to give the land made available to the peasants. He also favoured allowing workers to run their own factories. He also proposed to increase taxes on the wealthy and confiscate all the land owned by the Roman Catholic Church. It is not surprising that his party failed to win a single seat. In Milan, where Mussolini gained just over 2 per cent of the vote, his jubilant opponents staged a mock funeral. The funeral procession stopped outside his house and invited him to attend the funeral of his own party. Mussolini certainly had a need to re-think his party's policies but their celebrations about the demise of his party were to prove premature.

With an electoral system based on proportional representation, a system that allocated seats to parties according to their voting strength, it was always difficult to form a long-lasting and stable government in Italy. Since no single party was capable of winning an overall majority, governments came and went as the country was governed by one fragile coalition after another. Whilst the Christian Democrats refused to work with the Socialists and the Socialists refused to work with any party predominantly drawn from the middle classes, coalition governments seldom proved to be workable. Consequently during the period between July 1919 and October 1922, Italy had four different prime ministers each of which tried to survive on an uneasy alliance between the Christian Democrats and the Liberals. The series of short-lived coalitions caused people to wonder if Italy was becoming ungovernable.

Bienno Rosso – the 'Two Red Years'

During the period of unrest that followed the war, four prime ministers tried to restore political stability.

table 4 Italian prime ministers 1919–22	
Jun 1919–Jun 1920	Francisco Nitti
Jun 1920–Jun 1921	Giovanni Giolitti
Jun 1921–Feb 1922	Ivanoe Bonomi
Feb 1922–Oct 1922	Luigi Facta

In June 1919, Francisco Nitti, a former university lecturer and economist, became Prime Minister.

In an effort to restore some sort of order to the Italian political scene, he did his best to win the support of the Socialists for his moderate policies. Unfortunately, as the country's economic problems worsened with the rate of inflation increasing, prices rising, living standards falling and the value of people's savings becoming near worthless, they were in no mood to listen and the unrest continued. As major firms went bankrupt and unemployment soared to over 2 million so trade union membership rose to record levels. As is usually the case, poverty brought with it desperation and, in order to survive, many turned to crime so that theft and violence was out of control. During the year, millions of workers took part in demonstrations and strikes and Nitti's indecisive government appeared incapable of restoring order.

Across the countryside, peasants refused to harvest the crops and this endangered food supplies to the urban areas. Although the peasants did not generally approve of the Socialist plan to take all land into public ownership, some did take part in illegal land occupations. The interests of the peasants were safeguarded by Peasant Leagues, some of which were organized by the Socialists and others by the Catholic-dominated Christian Democrats. Both were capable of acts of terror as they burned down buildings, slaughtered animals, attacked the landlords and their agents and illegally occupied uncultivated land. The result was that many of the despairing landowners decided to call it a day, sell their holdings and get out whilst they could. To make the matter worse, when peasants who had earlier gone to find work in the towns returned to their villages, the Peasant Leagues ordered them to move on. With something like civil war raging in the countryside, Nitti's government seemed either unwilling or powerless to act. Pathetically, they issued decrees that gave official approval to the illegal acts.

With the peasantry running wild, it was only a matter of time before the industrial workers followed their example. During 1920, angered by the breakdown in their pay negotiations, workers in Bergamo became the first to occupy their factories. Urged on by the extreme trade unionists known as syndicalists that belonged to the *Unione Sindacale Italiana,* other workers in the industrial heartland in the north that included Milan, Turin and Genoa followed their example. Finally factory occupations spread to Rome, Florence, Naples and Palermo in southern Italy. Factory occupations were rather grand occasions that were accompanied by parades with the waving of red flags and music provided by workers' bands. In some factories, workers' councils were set up similar to the Soviet councils established in Russia by Lenin's Bolsheviks. Strictly speaking, factory occupations were not strikes since the workers continued to produce goods, besides which the support of sympathetic railway workers ensured that they were able to get their manufactured goods to market.

After a year in office, Nitti resigned and gave way to the 78-year-old veteran Giovanni Giolitti. The new Prime Minister adopted the negative policy of wait and see in the hope that as time passed the militancy of the workers would lessen and popular support for the Socialists and Communists would decline. Industrialists and those with commercial interests did not approve of this approach. Exasperated with Giolitti's indecisiveness, they recruited their own private armies to protect their land and businesses. In 1921, Giolitti finally gave up and resigned. The elections were preceded by a period of lawlessness as members of Mussolini's black-shirted Fascist *squadristi* went on the rampage and fought street battles against their political enemies, the Socialists, Communists and Anarchists. It is estimated that some 3,000 were killed during these savage encounters. In the provinces, Fascist *squadristi* went on so-called 'propaganda trips' where they ransacked and burned houses and forcibly removed Socialist councils and disbanded the Peasant Leagues. However, the violence was far from one-sided. In Milan, the Anarchists were responsible for the deaths of 18 people when they bombed a theatre. There was even an attempt to murder Mussolini by a young anarchist, Biagio Masi. Afterwards, the would-be assassin fled to Trieste where he was arrested. A feature of this period was that the police, military and the magistrates appeared to turn a blind eye to the Fascist outrages whilst some, clearly acting on orders from above, assisted the *squadristi* in their reign of terror.

A local government official appealed to the Prime Minister, described the situation and asked for help:

> Must report to your Excellency the very grave situation that has been created in the town of Budrio. Terrorised by an unpunished Fascist band using clubs, revolvers etc. Union organisers and municipal administrators forced to leave for fear of death. Workers forced to lock themselves at home because of continuous beatings and threats of beatings. Unions and socialist clubs ordered to dissolve themselves within 48 hours or face physical destruction. Life of the town paralysed, authorities powerless. Mass of workers request strong measures to protect their freedom of association and personal safety.
>
> (From Central State Archives Rome, 1921.)

Without becoming actively involved himself, Mussolini watched these outrages and presented himself as the only man capable of restoring law and order in Italy. Some believed him and an increasing number of normally law-abiding citizens turned to the Fascists to remedy the situation. In the election, the Socialists won 123 seats, the Christian Democrats 107 and the Communists only 15. The election result was also disappointing for Mussolini and his Fascists but with 35 seats in the Chamber of Deputies, the *Partito Nazionale Fascista* had at least some representation in the Chamber. Mussolini, who was elected deputy for Milan, assumed the leadership of the Party whilst other leading Fascists returned, included Dino Grandi, Cesare de Veechi and Roberto Farinacci.

Giolitti's successor, the moderate Socialist Ivanoe Bonomi, tried to form a government of Liberals and Christian Democrats. However, the elections had not brought an end to the violence and in the Chamber of Deputies, Fascist deputies forcibly removed a Socialist known to have been a wartime deserter whilst another Socialist deputy, Giacomo Matteotti bitterly complained at the harassment suffered by members of his party.

He expressed the view that in Italy 'private justice is in operation replacing public justice'. In an attempt to end the violence, the Pope called for a truce during Holy Week and Bonomi invited the various party leaders to a meeting. After some hesitation, Mussolini agreed to attend but the Communists and the Christian Democrats declined the invitation. At the meeting, the Fascists and Socialists agreed to a Treaty of Pacification and to bring to an end their on-going conflict. Unfortunately, the Fascists continued their acts of terrorism and some even spoke of replacing Mussolini as leader. In the end, the pressure told and the Fascist leader withdrew from the treaty.

After only ten months in office, Bonomi resigned and was replaced by Luigi Facta. The new Prime Minister fared no better and resigned but with no one willing to take his place, was immediately restored. On the very day that Facta formed his government, the Italian trade unions called for a general strike in protest at the violence used by the Fascist *squadrismo*. With the country now close to political breakdown and seemingly impossible to govern, it appeared that the only possible remedy was a period of totalitarian government. Mussolini and his Fascists had been waiting for such an opportunity but were the Italian people really willing to sacrifice their freedom in exchange for the order and discipline that might be enforced by dictatorial leadership?

05

the march on Rome and the Fascist coup of 1922

This chapter will cover:
- the outcome of the Fascist conference of 1921
- the Party's 'New Programme'
- the background to the march on Rome and its consequences
- the nature of Fascism and some definitions
- the extent and nature of Italian support for Fascism.

'This is our pledge: each day to love more deeply that adorable mother whose name is Italy.'

(From a speech by Benito Mussolini in 1921.)

The Fascist Party conference of 1921

figure 7 a poster advertising the third Party conference shows the new dynamic Fascism finally putting an end to the old, outdated Italy

The third Fascist Party conference held in November 1921 was of great significance since Mussolini used the occasion to formally turn his Fascist movement into a national political party. In each of the provinces, the party leader would be the *ras* and he was to have absolute power over Party members. Before being adopted by the Fascists, the term *ras* was applied to an Abyssinian prince. In order to gain popularity, Mussolini also ended his anti-Church stance and opposition to the monarchy. In a speech to the delegates, he said:

I do not regret that I was once a Socialist, I have burned all my bridges with the past and feel no nostalgia. Our aim is not to introduce socialism but leave it behind...One hears that the masses must be won over...we do indeed wish to serve them, to educate them but we also intend to flog them when they make mistakes. We want to raise their (the Italian people) intellectual and moral level in order to...introduce them to the history of the nation...At the same time we are hereby warning them that when the interests of the nation are at stake...the workers and middle classes must take a back seat...I urge all of you to remain faithful to Fascism.

The conference also considered and approved a lengthy policy document, the New Programme of the National Fascist Party. The main features of the programme may be summarized as follows:

- **Fascism** Fascism, as a political party, aimed to tighten its discipline and clarify its policies. The Nation, so it said, was 'not simply a sum of individual beings...it is the combination of all the values of the race'.
- **The State** The main function of the State was the preservation of political and judicial order. The citizens individual problems and problems that involved the national interest were to be the responsibility of Parliament.
- **The Church** The Church was not to infringe on the sovereignty of the State but must be allowed freedom 'to exercise its spiritual mission'.
- **Corporations** Corporations were to be set up to further national unity and to increase production. They were to be based on the principles of an eight-hour working day for all earners, the provision of social security for those injured at work, the sick and the old, worker representation in management and an improvement in the quality of management.
- **Domestic policy** The Party aimed to 'improve and dignify' the level of political behaviour so that public and private morality were of the same standard.
- **Foreign policy** Italy was to become 'the upholder of Latin civilisation in the Mediterranean' and firmly impose its authority over the various nationalities in the countries annexed to Italy.
- **Financial and economic policy** Public officials were to be held responsible for their actions and people would be

expected to fulfill their 'financial obligations' – pay their
taxes. Action was to be taken to protect Italian industry from
foreign competition. A new and simplified system of
collecting taxes was to be introduced. New public works
projects were to include the electrification of the railways,
extension of the road system and improved port facilities.
Mismanaged nationalized industries were to be returned to
private enterprise and the monopolies held by the post and
telegraph services were to end.

- **Social policy** The right to own private property was to be
  guaranteed. The conflict between different classes was to be
  brought to an end and strikes in the public services were to
  be prohibited.
- **Education policy** The struggle to eradicate illiteracy was to
  be intensified and the age of compulsory education extended.
  Schools were to provide adequate moral and physical
  education and teachers' pay improved.
- **Justice** Improved measures for dealing with juvenile
  delinquency and penalties for breaking the law to be both
  punishment and corrective training.
- **National defence** Every citizen would be expected to do
  compulsory military service.

From an Italian viewpoint, the appeal of the programme was
that it offered something for everyone whatever their status or
former party allegiance. However, the overall prospects for a
better future hid less appealing features – the implied supremacy
of the State over individual rights, the denial of the right to
strike and compulsory military service. Further, nowhere in the
programme were democratic government and the protection of
fundamental human rights mentioned.

The march on Rome

The decision of the Socialists to call a general strike was badly
conceived and played into Mussolini's hands. His reaction was
to order the *squadristi* into the towns and cities to terrorize the
workers and smash the strike. In Ancona, Leghorn and Genoa,
the headquarters of the Socialists were burned to the ground
and their printing presses destroyed. Afterwards, the Socialist
authorities in Milan were overthrown and the strike rapidly
brought to an end. On 24 October 1922, a triumphant
Mussolini addressed a large party gathering in the San Carlo
opera house in Naples:

Gentlemen, this problem has to be faced as a problem of force. Every time in history that strong clashes of interests and ideas occur, it is force that finally decides the matter. That is why we have gathered and powerfully equipped and resolutely disciplined our legions – so that if a clash must decide the matter on the level of force, victory will be ours. And now Fascists and citizens of Naples…It is good that we have been able to come to every corner of the land to get acquainted with you and see you as you are a courageous people, who face up to life's struggle Roman-style. Long live Italy! Long live Fascism!

At the end of the speech, the Fascist delegates rose to applaud and chant '*A Roma*', 'to Rome'. It was the outcome Mussolini dearly wanted. In Rome, a frantic Facta reshuffled his government and offered to include Fascists in his government but Mussolini was not prepared to accept a secondary role and declined the Prime Minister's offer. He told his supporters that he had no intention of coming to power 'by the servants' door' and instead made plans for a Fascist coup. His intention was to mass some 30,000 to 50,000 blackshirted Fascists at points outside the city and then converge on Rome. The furthest distance to be covered was 30 kilometres. The overall responsibility for the march was left to his lieutenants, a quadrumvirate of Italo Balbo, Michele Bianchi, Emilo De Bono and Cesare De Vecchi who were based at the Hotel Brufani in Perugia. Just before the march, they issued a proclamation:

Fascisti! Italians! The time for determined action has come…Today the army of Blackshirts seizes again the mutilated victory, and going directly to Rome, carries it back to the glories of the Capitol…The martial law of Fascism now becomes a fact…Following upon an order from the *Duce*, [(*Duce* (leader) was a title later assumed by Mussolini)], military, political and administrative powers are assumed by a quadrumvirate of action with dictatorial powers. The army, the safeguard of the nation, will not take part in this struggle…Fascism, furthermore, does not march against the police but against the political class both cowardly and imbecile, which in four long years has not been able to give a government to the nation… Fascists of all Italy! We must and shall win! Long live Italy! Long live Fascism!

In Rome, a desperate Facta urged Victor Emmanuel III to declare martial law and use the army to defend the city. However, the King realized that at best he could only muster

12,000 troops and was also aware that public opinion had turned in favour of the Fascists. Even though his military commander, General Badoglio, assured him that, if required, the army would restore order in no time, the King continued to dither. On the night of 27 October, Fascists began to take over strategic points – post offices, railway stations and government buildings – in towns and cities in northern and central Italy and the following morning, the columns began to converge on Rome. Mussolini had made his way back from Naples to the offices of his newspaper in Milan and remained close to the Swiss frontier just in case things went wrong and he had to make his escape.

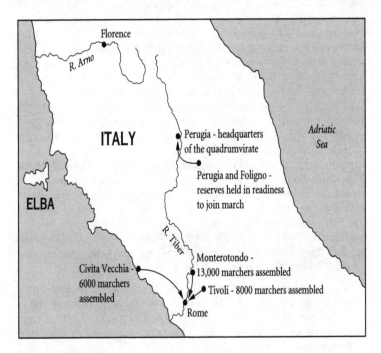

figure 8 the Fascist march on Rome

From the start, things began to go wrong for the marchers. In some areas, the railways had been sabotaged so that many marchers failed to reach their assembly points. Those who did appeared unimpressive since they were only armed with shotguns and farm implements. Heavy rain soon led to weariness and despondency so that enthusiasm for the march dwindled and some even dropped out. From his country home, Victor Emmanuel III, a man who had always behaved correctly and with dignity as a constitutional monarch and had previously shown no fondness for the Fascist movement, was in a difficult position. Within the royal family, he was aware that his mother, ex-Queen Margherita, sympathized with the Fascists, as did his cousin, the Duke of Aosta and there was always a chance that he might be forced to abdicate in favour of the personable duke. He was also aware that several of his generals favoured the Fascists and that some were actually taking part in the march. At all costs, the King wanted to avoid taking any action that might risk open conflict or even civil war. On returning to Rome, his first inclination was to declare martial law and prepare to defend the city. However, soon afterwards when a document authorizing such action was placed before him, he changed his mind and refused to sign. Victor Emmanuel's confused thinking handed what few advantages he had to Mussolini. He still hoped that the Fascist leader might be persuaded to serve in a government led by the country's wartime Prime Minister, Antonio Salandra, but now, brimming with confidence, Mussolini was prepared to accept nothing less than the premiership. Later that day, the King capitulated and invited the Fascist leader to form a government. Mussolini took an overnight train from Milan and arrived in Rome the following morning to a wildly enthusiastic reception. Against the King's wishes he, together with other leading Fascists and their supporters, celebrated their victory with a march through the city. Even though the Fascists still had only 35 Deputies in the Chamber, their takeover of the country was well under way. Speaking later that day, Mussolini said:

> My ancestors were peasants who tilled the earth and my father was a blacksmith who bent red-hot iron on the anvil. Sometimes when I was a boy, I helped my father in his hard and humble work, and now I have the infinitely harder task of bending souls.

The march on Rome was not such a glorious episode as may first appear since many of the marchers took the easy way and actually arrived in Rome by train. In retrospect, it is easy to see that Mussolini had pulled off a magnificent bluff since there can be little doubt that his actions could easily have been thwarted had the King called upon the Italian forces. Nevertheless, when Mussolini appeared before the King to be charged with the creation of a new government, he appeared in a black shirt and not the customary ceremonial uniform. The following morning, Mussolini wrote in the newspaper, *Il Popolo d'Italia*:

> A tremendous victory is in sight, with the almost unanimous approval of the nation. But victory is not to be mutilated by eleventh hour complications...Fascism wants power and will have it.

At 39 years of age, Mussolini had become Prime Minister, although the Fascist representation in the Chamber of Deputies was still only 35 Deputies, that represented less than 7 per cent of the total of 535. Put simply, a small minority group of bullies and murderers had taken over the government of Italy.

The appeal of Fascism

As we have seen, Fascism gained a dubious type of respectability when, during a period of industrial and rural strife, Mussolini appeared to champion law and order. In addition, by dropping their earlier republicanism and anti-Church stance, they were able to appeal to a broader section of the Italian people. The majority of people who came to support Fascism did not do so for reasons of a belief in a defined political theory but simply out of a longing for the restoration of stable government based on strong leadership, enforced law and order, social reform and improvements in the country's economic condition and their own family's standard of living. In other words, they supported Fascism because it was in their interests to do so. They hoped that after years of inept Liberal government, Fascism would bring about a national revival and a restoration of Italy's international prestige. In addition, industrialists, businessmen, the upper and middle classes and the Catholic Church thought that Fascism would frustrate the further spread of Marxist-inspired revolution and godless Communism. The popularity of Fascism was also the product of the excellent use of propaganda and the charisma and gifted oratory of Mussolini himself. Again, there is no doubt that fear of the gangs of Blackshirt thugs, the *squadrismo*, also played a part.

Support for Fascism

Eventually, support for Fascism came from a wide spectrum of Italian society. Of course, the central pillar of support came from the fanatics who had marched and demonstrated as

Blackshirts and as armed irregulars, the *squadristi*, had fought in the streets and terrorized their opponents. As we have seen, those whose best interests were served by supporting Fascism included industrialists, bankers and businessmen who feared the advance of Communism, and many of the upper and middle classes particularly businessmen, artisans, traders and shopkeepers. The peasantry also recognized the Communist threat to take over their lands and saw it as a good reason to support the Fascists. The Roman Catholic Church in the form of a new Pope, Pius XI, was opposed to Marxist atheism. Ex-soldiers and nationalists generally recognized that the Fascists were the most likely to redress the terms of the 'mutilated victory' that followed the First World War and now that Mussolini had abandoned republicanism, many monarchists gave their support to the Fascists. The ranks of the Fascists also included many young people – idealistic students and young hooligans who had thrived on street violence and intimidation.

table 5 membership of the Italian Fascist Party in 1921

Profession or occupation	Number	Percentage of total
Industrialists	4,269	2.8
Landowners	18,094	12.1
Professional (doctors, solicitors, etc.)	9,981	6.6
Tradesmen and artisans	13,979	9.3
Private employees	14,989	9.8
Public employees	7,209	4.8
Teachers	1,668	1.2
Students	19,783	13.2
Industrial workers	23,410	15.6
Agricultural workers	36,874	24.6

(Source: *Il Partito Nazionale Fascista*, 1935.)

Some definitions of Fascism

Before we go further, it is best that we consider exactly what is meant by the term Fascist or fascism. The origin of the word Fascist is said to derive from the Latin *fasces*, a bundle of rods with an axe projecting which, in the days of Ancient Rome, was carried by a lector, the person who walked ahead of the chief magistrate. Mussolini was very conscious of Italy's past and it was natural that he should use a Latin term as the name for his political philosophy and party.

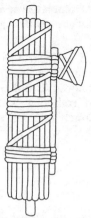

figure 9 the *fasces*, a symbol of Ancient Rome

The definition of fascism that appears in the *Chambers dictionary* reads 'A form of authoritarian government in Italy 1922–1943 characterised by extreme nationalism, militarism, anti-communism and restrictions on individual freedom.' The Oxford and other dictionaries are a little less specific – 'An authoritarian or totalitarian political system characterised by aggressive nationalism and the absolute sovereignty off the state over individual rights and interests.' As you might expect, dictionaries used in the former Soviet Union saw things differently, 'The most reactionary and openly terroristic form of the dictatorship of finance capitalism established by imperialistic bourgeoisie to break the resistance of the working class and all progressive elements in society.' When Mussolini was asked to define Fascism, he replied 'Fascism is too subtle a body of ideas to be understood by laymen and foreigners'. However, in an essay on the nature of Fascism, he later provided a more direct and less defensive definition:

> ...the Fascist system of life stresses the importance of the State and recognises the individual only in so far as his interests coincide with those of the state...Fascism stands for liberty and for the only liberty worth having, the liberty of the State and of the individual within the State. The Fascist conception of the State is all embracing; outside of it no human or spiritual values may exist, much less have any value. Thus understood, Fascism is totalitarian...

Historians and political theorists offer varying definitions of Fascism. In a lecture entitled *Che cosa e il fascismo*? (What is

Fascism?), the Italian scholar Giovanni Gentile, the so-called 'Philosopher of Fascism', provides a profound if weighty definition:

> Fascism is a party and political doctrine. But Fascism...is above all a total conception of life. It is impossible to be a Fascist in politics and not in school, not in one's family and office...Thus Fascism embodies what may be called its own characteristic, namely taking life seriously. Life is toil, effort, sacrifice and hard work; a life in which we know perfectly well there is neither matter nor time for amusement.

Later, Mussolini appointed Gentile to be his Minister of Education.

The *Enciclopedia Italiana* saw Fascist doctrine as being:

> ...the idea of the State its nature, its function and its objectives. For Fascism the State is an absolute, thus individuals and groups only have an existence in relation to it...Fascist thinking is wholly committed to the State...Fascism supports the only liberty that can be a serious thing, that is the liberty of the State and of the individual within the State...nothing can exist outside the State.
>
> (*Enciclopedia Italiana* XIV, 1932.)

Non-Italian historians and political theorists are more matter-of-fact in their definitions. The historian Denis Mack Smith gives an idea of Mussolini's contradictory views and questions whether or not he had any clearly defined political views at all.

> Fascism, he (Mussolini) sometimes said was not a doctrine, but a technique; it was a means to get power. Oddly enough, the basic question whether Fascism was something of the left or of the right is still sometimes in doubt because it had elements of both... It was revolutionary but could also sometimes claim to be conservative. It was Monarchist but also Republican, at different times. It was Catholic but also anti-clerical, it claimed to be socialist but could also be strongly capitalist whenever it suited Duce to be so. There were no consistent ideas of Fascism, I think that Mussolini had no sincere beliefs at all...
>
> (From a lecture given by Denis Mack Smith that appeared in the *Modern History Review*, 1990.)

Another leading authority, Roger Griffin, has defined Fascism as:

> ...a modern political ideology that seeks to regenerate the social, economic and cultural life of a country by basing it on a heightened sense of national belonging and ethnic identity. Fascism rejects liberal ideas such as freedom and individual rights... Despite the idealistic goals of Fascism, attempts to build Fascist societies have led to wars and persecutions that caused millions of deaths, As a result, Fascism is associated with right-wing fanaticism, racism, totalitarianism, and violence.
>
> (From *Fascism* by Roger Griffin, Oxford University Press, 1995.)

Stuart Woolf offers another definition of Fascism:

> A dictatorial system of government, with popular appeal and substructure, which served to establish, strengthen or maintain a substantially capitalist economy against the real or imagined threat of a socialist take-over, invasion or revolution.
>
> (From *The Nature of Fascism* by Stuart Woolf, 1968.)

So where do these views leave us? Although the various interpretations of Fascism may sometimes be contradictory, there are features that remain constant. As we shall see in the coming chapters, Italian Fascism was a one-party dictatorship that was both militaristic and nationalistic. Above all, it was intolerant of civil and human rights and demanded the obedience and conformity of the Italian people. In all matters, the State was to exercise supremacy over the individual.

Finally, perhaps there is more truth than intended in the humorous comments made to illustrate the essential differences between the various political systems:

Capitalism	'You have two cows. You sell one and buy a bull.'
Communism	'You have two cows. The government takes them both and gives you some milk.'
Nazism	'You have two cows. The government takes them both and shoots you.'
Socialism	'You have two cows. The government takes one and gives it to your neighbour.'
Fascism	'You have two cows. The government takes them both and sells you the milk.'

06

towards a totalitarian dictatorship

This chapter will cover:
- the changes to the Italian constitution
- the first steps taken towards establishing a Fascist dictatorship
- the importance of the Fascist Grand Council
- the opposition to Fascism and the Matteotti crisis
- the Aventine Succession and its consequences
- the influence of Fascism on the Italian people.

'I could have transformed this grey assembly hall into an armed camp of Fascists. I could have nailed up the doors of Parliament.'

> (From the first speech made by Mussolini to the Chamber of Deputies in November 1922.)

Mussolini rigs the electoral system

When Benito Mussolini was first appointed Prime Minister of Italy in October 1922, his power base was extremely limited. In the Chamber, there were 35 Fascist Deputies and these represented only 7 per cent of the total membership. Clearly he had no chance of using democratic means to achieve his aims. In order to establish a Fascist dictatorship, he would need to move slowly and cautiously and be prepared to use both stealth and terror. Apart from the broadest and often vague definitions of the aims of Fascism, Mussolini had few detailed policies of his own. However, on one point he was absolutely certain and that was the correctness of his view regarding the relationship between the State and its citizens. This was well illustrated in a popular Fascist slogan of the time – 'Everything within the State, nothing against the State, nothing outside the State'. In other words, in all matters the position of the State was of unquestioned supremacy over the individual rights of its citizens. Other aspects of his domestic policy were also part of his plan to establish a totalitarian state. He urged employers and employees to work in harmony in the interests of the State and he also aimed to achieve *autarky*, Italian self-sufficiency in food and essential raw materials. As far as foreign policy was concerned, his aim was to seek national glory by showing greater resolve and, if necessary, through the use of aggression. Of course, one major difficulty was that neither Mussolini nor any of his Fascist colleagues had any previous experience of government.

On first coming to power, Mussolini first headed a coalition government made up of Social Democrats, Christian Democrats, Liberals and Fascists but of a Cabinet totalling 14 only four were Fascists. In order to gain as much power for himself as possible, he took over three Cabinet positions himself so that as well as being President of the Council, he took charge of both domestic and foreign affairs. Other Fascist ministers in the Cabinet included Aldo Oviglio as Minister of Justice, Alberto de Stefani as Minister of Finance whilst Giovanni

Giuriati was made responsible for the so-called Liberated Provinces, the northern provinces gained by Italy after the First World War. A new position of Director-General of Public Safety was created for Emilio De Bono. Since the old general and veteran Fascist had already gained something of a reputation for his leadership of the thugs of the *squadristi*, his appointment was regarded as a veiled threat to those likely to oppose the Fascists. At first, Mussolini appeared to be placatory and conciliatory and, although very much in control, he recognized the need to show moderation by creating a good image at home and abroad. He took no immediate steps against his political opponents and restored offices and presses to the political parties he had previously suppressed. Mussolini went further and as a gesture of goodwill to the Church, he abandoned his previous anti-Catholic stance and made a generous grant to increase the stipends paid to the clergy. He also ordered the restoration of the teaching of religious education in schools and colleges, banned obscene publications and declared swearing in public and the sale of contraceptives to be crimes. All this was clearly intended to win the support of Roman Catholics. However, his moderate and restrained policies hid an ulterior motive that was made evident when he next sought a vote of confidence and an agreement from the Italian parliament to grant him emergency powers for a year. In a lengthy speech that contained platitudes and concessions as well as implied threats, he said:

> Gentlemen, what I am doing now is a mark of respect towards you for which I ask no special recognition. For many years, too many years, government crises were made and solved by the Chamber by means of convoluted manoeuvres and scheming, so much that a crisis was usually called an attack and a ministry represented as a tottering stagecoach...I am here to defend and enforce in the highest degree the revolution of the Blackshirts, injecting them intimately into the history of the nation as a force for development, progress and stability...I told myself that the best wisdom is the wisdom that does not abandon one after the victory. With three thousand youths fully armed, fully determined and ready to act on any command of mine, I could have chastised all those who have denigrated and tried to harm Fascism...I could have removed Parliament and constructed a government exclusively of Fascists but I did not want to, at least for the present. I have formed a coalition government, not with

the intention of having a parliamentary majority that I can
do very well without, but in order to call to the aid of a
gasping nation as many as are willing to save the nation...I
believe that I also interpret the thought of the assembly
and certainly the majority of the Italian people in
expressing warm devotion to the Sovereign, who refused to
listen to the useless reactionaries and avoided civil
war...All the problems of the Italian people have been
solved on paper, but there has been a lacking to translate
them into fact. The government today represents this firm
and decisive will...We demand full powers because we
want to assume full responsibility...I do not intend to
exclude voluntary co-operation, which we will accept
gratefully whether it comes from Deputies, Senators or
competent private citizens.

Deputies must clearly have got the message, it was simply do as
I say and co-operate or prepare to be removed! The veteran, 81-
year-old and still respected Giolitti was certainly impressed with
what he heard and gave his immediate backing to Mussolini
when he said 'The country needs strong government and looks
beyond living from day to day...I fully approve of the speech
made by the Prime Minister.' As a result, when the vote of
confidence was held, the Italian parliament voted by 306 to 116
votes to grant Mussolini the emergency powers he requested.
Such was the enthusiasm that five former prime ministers –
Giolitti, Salandra, Orlando, Bonomi and Facta – all voted for
the measure that was in effect a betrayal of Italian democracy
since it, to all intents and purposes, granted Mussolini
dictatorial powers.

Immediately, the Fascist leader's brother, Arnaldo, was
appointed editor of *Il Popolo d'Italia*, the Party newspaper,
Fascist hoodlums previously imprisoned for their murderous
activities were pardoned and released and student activists who
had been detained or wounded received their degrees without
taking examinations. In December 1922, Mussolini created the
Gran Consiglio or Fascist Grand Council.

The *Gran Consiglio* – the Fascist Grand Council

The Fascist Grand Council was to be the main policy-making
body and the highest authority in the Fascist Party. Mussolini
nominated the 22 members of the Council and they met once a

month. It was his intention that the Grand Council, made up of a group of high ranking and dedicated Fascists, should act as a link between the Party and the government. It was to discuss and approve government policy and place its proposals first before the Cabinet and then parliament. In effect, the task of introducing new government policy was taken from parliament and handed to a group of Fascists whose only purpose was to further the interests of the Party.

Since Mussolini nominated the Council and it owed him total allegiance, its function was really to rubber stamp his decisions. Even so, its establishment represented a major step towards the Fascist leader establishing his dictatorship. As we shall see, as his own dictatorial powers increased so he became less dependent on the Council and its meetings occurred less frequently and when they did, Mussolini dominated the proceedings. He ignored its advice until in 1928 it finally lost its importance when it became simply one of the institutions of government. Early in 1923, Mussolini shrewdly took measures to give the *squadristi* some respectability when it assumed the grand title of *Milizia volontaria per la sicurezza nationale* – the Voluntary Fascist Militia for National Security. Although its methods and practices changed little, it was now a paid, full-time militia and its members took an oath of loyalty to Mussolini and not the King. Mussolini's next major step towards establishing his dictatorship was to change the electoral system so that it worked to the advantage of the Fascist Party.

The Acerbo Law of 1923

In was Giacomo Acerbo, a Fascist under-secretary, who proposed a law that, apart from the fact parliamentary elections were still to be based on proportional representation, was to completely change the old electoral system. As part of measures described by Mussolini as 'the most Fascist of reforms', the country was to be divided into 15 large constituencies and in each constituency, the various political parties had to submit a list of candidates. In future general elections, any party gaining 25 per cent or more of the votes would automatically be allocated two-thirds of the seats in the Chamber of Deputies. The remainder of the seats would be divided between the other parties. The Socialists, Communists and Liberals immediately rejected Acerbo's proposals but with Mussolini's ex-*squadristi* militiamen close at hand, many of the law's opponents backed down and the measure was passed by 223 votes to 123. Once in effect, Mussolini ordered the existing Chamber of Deputies to be dissolved and elections held under the new rules in April 1924.

The problems of establishing a Fascist dictatorship were not the only ones that faced the Prime Minister. Mussolini also had to keep a wary eye on the activities of the *ras* in the provinces. Some, particularly Roberto Faranacci, were becoming increasingly troublesome as they demanded even more positive action and a decisive move to the extreme right in Italian politics. In many provincial towns, the *ras* had already acted independently and forcibly removed freely elected councils and replaced them with Fascist administrations.

The elections of 1924

Before the elections took place and clearly as a tactical move aimed at ensuring a Fascist victory, Mussolini brought about the merger of the Fascist and other right-wing nationalist political parties. With the opposition parties hopelessly divided and unwilling to join together in a common front, the elections were held in an atmosphere of unmatched fear, intimidation and violence. Fascist militia quite openly roamed the streets arresting thousands of their Party's opponents. Many were badly beaten and some, including a Socialist candidate, were murdered. In addition, the Italian people were subjected to a massive propaganda campaign whilst the opposition press was carefully watched and its access to the media strictly limited. Corruption was everywhere and the militia, ever in attendance at the polling booths, threatened the electorate as they encouraged them to make the right decision and so it became prudent and certainly safer to support the Fascists. The malpractice did not end there since ballot boxes were lost and there were obvious and blatant discrepancies in the counting of the votes. In some constituencies, the Fascists did not even attempt to cover the fact that the elections were rigged. With so much corruption and pressure on the electorate, the outcome of the election was never really in doubt and few were surprised that 66 per cent of the people voted for Mussolini's Fascists. With their right-wing allies, the Fascists gained 374 of the 535 seats in the Chamber and it is perhaps surprising that so many people still had the courage to vote for the opposition parties.

table 6 the general election of 1924	
Fascists and their Nationalist supporters	374
Christian Democrats (often referred to as *Populari*)	39
Socialists	24
Communists	19
Various others	79

An analysis of the results showed that the Fascists had been particularly strong in Romagna, Tuscany, parts of the Po valley and the south where they had gained 80 per cent or more of the votes. In the north, however, they had only managed to win slightly more than half the votes and in some big cities and the industrial areas they were still in a minority.

With an overall average of 65 per cent of the votes and the opposition parties reduced to a bunch of quarrelling and ineffectual bunglers, it is possible to wonder if the earlier commotion about the Acerbo Law was really worthwhile. However, there were still a few with the courage to voice their concern about Mussolini's tactics. One of the most outspoken in his criticism was Giacomo Matteotti, the 39-year-old rising star of the Socialist Party.

The Matteotti crisis

Giacomo Matteotti was born in 1885, the son of a wealthy landowner in the Rivigo region of Italy. It was during his years as a law student that he first became actively involved in Socialist politics and had opposed Italy's involvement in the First World War. His particular brand of socialism was of the moderate, non-militant variety but because of his reputation as a pacifist many considered him defeatist and unreliable. In 1924, he was appointed secretary of the Unitary Socialist Party and his gifted and spirited oratory soon earned him the nickname, 'the Tempest'.

He was certainly no coward and his book, *The Fascists Exposed*, attempted to draw to the attention of the general public the grim reality of Mussolini's methods. In this book, he had the courage to write '...never as in the last year, during which Fascism has been in power, has the law been so thrust aside in favour of arbitrary action, the State so subjugated by a faction, or the nation split into two classes, the dominating and the subject class'. During the election of 1924, he was one of the Socialist candidates attacked and beaten by the *squadristi* now masquerading as the Voluntary Fascist Militia. Even after their overwhelming victory, Matteotti continued to rant against the Fascists and in two-hour speech in the Chamber listed their abuses of power and demanded that the elections should be declared invalid. As tempers rose, Deputies stood and tried to silence him with shouts of 'We will teach you respect with a shot in the back' and 'Go to Russia'. Matteotti responded 'You may kill me but you will never kill my ideas. The workers will bless my corpse…Long live Socialism.' As some Deputies turned and walked out, Matteotti turned to his friends and said, 'Now you can start drafting my funeral oration.' Throughout, Mussolini had sat stony faced and in silence but was later known to have commented 'that man should no longer be in circulation'. Five days later, Matteotti resumed his attack on the Fascists but this time Mussolini stood to reply. He accused the Socialist deputy of presenting a one-sided argument and pointed out that several Fascists had also been killed and wounded during the election campaign. He concluded with a warning, 'In Russia, you would have been shot. There is still time.'

On 10 July 1924, five men seized Matteotti as he left his apartment in the Lungo Tevere Arnaldo da Bresica. They bundled him into a waiting Lancia car and as he struggled to escape, he was stabbed repeatedly. It was the intention of the gang leader, Amerigo Dumini, to drive to some distance to Tuscany and bury him where his body would not easily be found. Unfortunately, other members of his gang panicked and after driving around aimlessly for some hours, placed their victim's body in a shallow grave a short distance from Rome. As a search was mounted, Matteotti's wife went to see Mussolini and demanded to know what had become of her husband. Two days later, the Prime Minister addressed Parliament:

I believe that the Chamber is concerned with what has happened to Deputy Matteotti, who disappeared suddenly on Tuesday afternoon at a time and in circumstances that are uncertain but can support the view that a crime has been committed, can only arouse the indignation and the grief of the government and Parliament.

The following day, a number of opposition Deputies withdrew from Parliament in what became known as the Aventine Secession.

The Aventine Succession

The Deputies concerned in the withdrawal from Parliament were copying the action taken in 500 BC by a less privileged section of the people of Ancient Rome, the plebs, when they withdrew from the city to the nearby Aventine Hill in protest at the dominance of the patricians, the Roman aristocracy. Their aim was to have a greater say in the government. In 1924, the Aventines, as the Deputies were known, met away from the Chamber in order to watch the turn of events from a distance and put pressure on the Prime Minister to deal with the perpetrators of the crime. A few even considered calling for a general strike and even proclaiming themselves to be the legal government of Italy. In reality, they were playing into Mussolini's hands since their absence from the Chamber made his position even stronger.

The following month, Matteotti's naked and mutilated body was discovered in a shallow grave on wasteland just 20 kilometres outside Rome. Mussolini immediately claimed that he knew nothing of the killing and although a number of subsequent inquiries were held, no positive evidence came to light to prove that he had ordered the murder. On the other hand, his innocence remains far from certain and many historians are of the opinion that he was certainly involved. However, there is evidence that implicates other leading members of the Fascist Party. Amerigo Dumini was a known gangster and was given to boasting of the number of assassinations he had committed whilst other members of his gang – Augusto Malacria, Amieto Poveromo, Giuseppe Viola and Albini Volpi – were little more than small-time crooks. All had once been members of the *squadristi* that had formed a group of murderous assassins that took its name from Lenin's infamous secret police in Bolshevik Russia, the *Cheka*. There were numerous witnesses to the abduction of Matteotti and the car involved, found with bloodstained seats, was owned by Filippo Filippelli, a close friend of Mussolini and the editor of the Fascist newspaper, *Corriere Italiano*. There was also evidence of the involvement of members of the Fascist Grand Council, Cesare Rossi and Filippo Marinelli.

Mussolini's reaction was to express his horror at the atrocity and convey his condolences to Matteotti's wife and two young sons. He vehemently denied that the murder was part of a Fascist conspiracy and promised to ruthlessly hunt down the killers and provide the victim's family with a pension. In the

Chamber, he said 'If there is anyone in this room who more than all the rest, has the right to be angry, it is I. Only one of my enemies could commit this crime that fills us with horror and stirs us to cries of anger.'

Dumini was arrested at the railway station as he attempted to leave Rome whilst Filippelli, Rossi and Marinelli were also taken into custody. Under cross-examination, Dumini admitted to killing Matteotti and the other three confessed to being implicated in the crime. The extenuating circumstances, so they claimed, was the fact that they were sure that Mussolini wanted the Socialist Deputy eliminated. Brought to trial, all four men were found guilty but treated leniently since they claimed they were provoked when Matteotti resisted their attempt to kidnap him! Sentenced to six years' imprisonment, they were released after two when Marinelli resumed his place on the Fascist Grand Council. Interestingly, after the Second World war when Marinelli was awaiting execution for other crimes, he stated that Mussolini had not known of the plan to murder Matteotti and that he had arranged it without his leader's knowledge. However, the repercussions that followed the murder of the Deputy were far from over.

figure 10 a cartoon that appeared in the Italian newspaper, *Becco Giallo*, in 1924
© Topham Picturepoint

Whether or not Mussolini knew of it, from his point of view, the murder of Matteotti was a major blunder. In the Chamber, the Fascist Deputies refuted all the accusations made against their Party whilst the King, Victor Emmanuel III, realizing that his own position depended on Mussolini's patronage even refused to consider the documentary evidence relating to the case. Nevertheless, across the country there was a widespread belief that Mussolini was responsible or at very least had prior knowledge of the murder. There was a public outcry followed by a wave of unrest that included protests and even anti-Fascist demonstrations in the streets. Many ex-servicemen and even a number of Fascists expressed their concern with a few even tearing up their party membership cards. Former prime ministers such as Orlando and Giolitti began to reconsider their support for Mussolini. The Fascist leader seemed uncertain how to react and there is some reason to believe that at this stage a coup against him might have won the support of the majority of Italians and been successful. However, his opponents dithered for too long and gave Mussolini time to recover. Mussolini was not totally without support and some came from the most unexpected quarters:

> The London *Times* condemned the murder of Matteotti...but hastened to add that it would be very wrong for the opposition in Italy to bring down Mussolini's government. The *Times* was certain that Mussolini would handle the situation 'in the right way'...The *Daily Mail* hailed Mussolini as 'the Saviour of Italy' and declared: 'We have every confidence in Signor Mussolini; so have the Italians'. Ramsay MacDonald (the British Prime Minister) unwittingly helped Mussolini by agreeing a treaty ceding Jubaland to Italy. The agreement was initialled at the Foreign Office on 9th June 1924, the day before Matteotti was murdered. The news of this diplomatic success came just at the right time to help Mussolini during the furore about the murder.
>
> (From *Mussolini* by Jasper Ridley, Constable 1997.)

In order to buy time and appease his critics, Mussolini made some concessions by sacking De Bono as Chief of Police and handing over his own responsibilities for domestic affairs to Luigi Federzoni. On the other hand, there were those extremists within his own party, particularly the *ras*, who urged him to pull himself together and take more positive action. Even though further damning evidence came to light when the newspaper *Il Mondo* published a confession made by Cesare Rossi that implicated Mussolini, it was clear that the Fascist leader was likely to survive the storm. The truth was that as long as the threat of Communism existed, those with vested interests – the industrialists, businessmen, landowners, the upper classes, the army and the Church – would continue to support Mussolini. Why? Simply because their fear of Bolshevism was greater than their fear of Fascism.

It was not until January 1925 that Mussolini felt confident enough to turn on his accusers. In a speech to the Chamber of Deputies:

> I tell you here, in the presence of this assembly and before the whole Italian people, that I alone assume the moral and historical responsibility for what has happened...If Fascism has been a criminal plot, if violence has resulted from a certain historic, political and moral atmosphere, the responsibility is mine, because I have deliberately created this atmosphere...Now the time for faint heartedness is passed...the Aventine sedition has born consequences...a revival of Communism, but Fascism, at once a party and a government, is at the height of its power and so the moment comes to say enough...Gentlemen of the Aventine, you have deluded yourselves...

As usual, he ended his speech with an implied threat:

> Italy wants peace and quiet work and calm. I will give these things with love if possible, and with force if necessary...You may be sure that within the next forty-eight hours everything will be clarified.

By confronting those who had turned against him, Mussolini's speech was a decisive moment in the history of Fascist rule in Italy. It signalled the start of an on-going process that would finally turn Italy into a totalitarian state.

The end of parliamentary democracy

During 1925 and 1926, Mussolini had manipulated the electoral system to his advantage, given the *squadristi* the appearance of respectability and managed to survive the crisis that followed the murder of the Socialist Deputy, Matteotti. Now he was in a position to finally overthrow what remained of Italian democracy and extinguish the civil liberties of the Italian people.

For the best part of two years Mussolini had tolerated the existence of opposition parties and even included their representatives in his coalition government but this was a sham democracy. In fact, the Fascists had already been passing laws by decree without reference to Parliament and now he was in a position to take steps to rid himself of the opposition. Early in 1925, he appointed the most radical and ruthless of the Fascist hierarchy, Roberto Farinacci, as Secretary of the Party. At the Party Congress later that year it was decided to ignore the opposition and disregard any protests that followed. The summer months saw a return of unrestricted Fascist violence as members of the opposition parties were beaten, killed or forced to seek exile abroad.

Then, after a call for greater discipline 'in the name of our beloved *Duce* and his deputy Farinacci' the violence subsided and there was a return to near normality. Finally in December, the last vestige of parliamentary democracy disappeared with the passing of the Law on the Power of the Head of Government by which Mussolini took the title Head of Government and was only accountable to the King. He now had the sole responsibility for introducing new legislation and any other proposals had to be submitted to him so that in effect he now officially had the power to rule by decree. At the same time, the Socialist Party, Matteotti's former party, was banned and soon afterwards the ban was extended to all opposition parties said to be 'obstructive rather than constructive'. Anyone found guilty of offending the honour or prestige of the Head of Government became liable to a five-year prison sentence whilst anyone involved in anti-Fascist activity could be deprived of their Italian citizenship. Parliamentary government was now a thing of the past and Italy was a totalitarian state run by one man, Benito Mussolini.

Other steps taken towards the establishment of a totalitarian state

The Fascists next moved to remove the opposition parties from holding office in local government. This was confirmed in 1926 when nominated Fascist officials replaced the few remaining elected local leaders. Elected mayors were removed and their places taken by *podesta*, a Fascist appointed local government official.

Up to this time, Socialist and Catholic trade unions, although subject to close scrutiny and with their activities limited, had been allowed to continue but now the Fascists set up their own unions or syndicates and the existing workers' organizations were banned. Fascist syndicates were intended to represent the interests of both employers and workers and by the Vidoni Palace Pact of 1925, both agreed to be represented solely by Fascist syndicates. This agreement, the Law of Corporations, abolished the right of workers to strike and of employers to lock out their workers. As we shall see, Mussolini's ultimate aim was to group all Italian industries into nine confederations.

Other associations, political and otherwise, were placed under close surveillance and many had their funds confiscated and their premises closed. A law, which was clearly aimed at Italian Freemasonry, prohibited secret societies. Fascists were not allowed to be Freemasons and in the end they were declared illegal and their lodges disbanded.

Until 1925, Mussolini had been prepared to tolerate some limited freedom of the press but only the boldest of newspaper owners allowed their editors to be critical of the Fascists. Strangely, and even though they caused the authorities some embarrassment, cartoons and articles were still allowed to appear in satirical magazines. The Fascists first tried to curb the freedom of the press by buying out the independent newspapers and appointing pro-Fascist editors to run them. All this half-hearted censorship finally came to an end in 1925 when all independent newspapers were closed and their editors arrested. Afterwards, the Interior Minister, Luigi Federzoni, finally brought the freedom of the press to an end by vigorously applying the new Press Laws that insisted that all views expressed in newspapers had to be pro-Fascist.

Attempts on Mussolini's life

Although the evidence of the 1924 elections suggests that the Fascist takeover of Italy had the overwhelming approval of the people, the next four years witnessed no less than four attempts on the life of Mussolini. The first came as early as November 1924 when Tito Zaniboni, a Socialist Deputy, made plans to shoot him when he appeared on the balcony of the Foreign Office in Rome. Foolishly, he boasted of his intentions to friends who betrayed his confidence and informed the police. Moments before Mussolini appeared, Zaniboni was arrested by the police and subsequently sentenced to 30 years' imprisonment. In 1926, it was a British woman, the Honourable Violet Gibson who made the second attempt on the Fascist leader's life. An eccentric member of the Anglo-Irish aristocracy and sister of Lord Ashbourne, she fired a shot at Mussolini that grazed his nose as he went to his car after opening an international medical congress in Rome. Arrested by the OVRA, the Italian secret police, her interrogation produced no evidence that connected her with any political group. The authorities accepted that the poor woman was mentally unstable and she was released and deported. Later in the same year, Gino Lucetti, a stone mason and self-confessed anarchist, threw a bomb at Mussolini's car. Although *Il Duce* escaped unharmed, several onlookers were wounded. Sentenced to 30 years' imprisonment, he was released in 1943 only to be killed during an Allied air raid. Finally, a 16-year-old youth, Anteo Zamboni, apparently on his own initiative decided to try his luck during a visit made by Mussolini to Bologna. In order to get close to his intended victim, he dressed in the uniform of a member of a Fascist youth movement. Zamboni fired at the Prime Minister's passing car but missed only to be seized and lynched by an outraged mob who literally tore him limb from limb. Later, his arms and legs were carried around the city and put on display by local Fascists. A great deal of mystery surrounded the incident. No witnesses came forward to identify Zamboni and some have claimed that he was only an innocent bystander. Others have suggested that he was an unfortunate pawn in a plot to stir up concern about public safety. It certainly provided the Fascists with yet another excuse to take steps to intensify Mussolini's dictatorship. A new law regarding public safety was passed and a tribunal set up to deal with those thought to be a threat to society and a risk to the state.

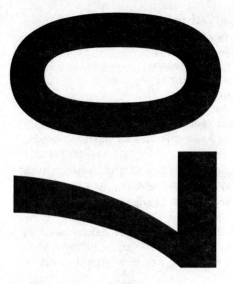

07

the early years of the Fascist dictatorship

This chapter will cover:
- Mussolini, his character –
  the man and the myth, his
  family and his lifestyle
- other leading Fascists
- the Fascists in control –
  Party and Parliament
- Mussolini and Victor
  Emmanuel III
- the continuing opposition to
  Fascism and its repression
- the strengths and
  weaknesses of Mussolini's
  Fascist regime.

'The poets and craftsmen,
The gentry and the peasants,
With the pride of Italians,
Swear loyalty to Mussolini.
There is no poor district
Which does not send its tale,
Which does not unfurl its banners
Of Fascism the redeemer.'
(From a Fascist hymn that often replaced
the national anthem.)

In 1940, United Artists made a film that was a satire based on
the life of Adolf Hitler, *The Great Dictator*. In the film, Charlie
Chaplin appeared in the role that was supposedly the German
dictator, whilst Jack Oakie played Benito Mussolini. In his
caricature of *Il Duce*, Oakie portrayed him as a clown and a fat,
jabbering buffoon and was nominated for an Academy Award.
Did Oakie do Mussolini justice and just how accurate was his
portrayal?

Benito Mussolini – the man and the myth

Many historians have attempted to draw comparisons between
Benito Mussolini and the two other infamous dictators of the
period, Adolf Hitler and Josef Stalin. Compared with the others
the Italian dictator was an also-ran and by no means a wholly
loathsome character. It is true that Mussolini was exceptionally
vain and at times his behaviour and actions appeared absurd
but, on the other hand in company whilst he always tried to
impress, he could also be charming and good-humoured.
Because of his background, he lacked the social graces and his
table manners often left a lot to be desired but over the years
these improved. In appearance, he was barely 1.7 metres tall
and of stocky build with a rapidly receding hairline. He always
seemed conscious of his appearance and physical condition and
his style of dress was very conservative – usually a plain suit and
tie and sometimes a butterfly collar and spats on his shoes.
Later, he took to always appearing in Fascist-style uniform. His
girth betrayed the fact that he took regular exercise and his diet
largely consisted of health foods and fruit juices. In the army, he
had been a heavy smoker but gave up the habit; he rarely
consumed alcohol and coffee. Even so, in the mid-1920s, he
suffered from stomach cramps and ulcers and briefly retired
from public life. There were rumours that the real cause of his

condition was the consequence of years suffering from venereal disease. He usually rose at 8 a.m. and after an afternoon rest, finally retired at 10 p.m. each evening. Much of his time was taken up attending meetings, conferences and receptions. A private man, Mussolini was not keen on being exposed to the glare of public life but preferred to be at his home, the Villa Torlonia, with his wife, Rachele, and their children where the family lived comfortably on the Prime Minister's salary. He was little concerned with the trappings of high office and liked to spend his weekends in the country away from affairs of state. He was quite a well-read man who spoke French fluently and English reasonably well. When he travelled he went either by chauffeur-driven car or special train and he also held a pilot's licence and occasionally piloted his aircraft himself. As we have seen, Mussolini, who once boasted that he made no friends in his life, enjoyed a very private life and disliked entertaining. However, there were those he welcomed to his home and these included Ezio Garibaldi, grandson of the patriot, the Polish-born biographer, Emil Ludwig, and his own brother, Arnaldo. Garibaldi, unlike the flatterers around him, told him the truth about the feelings of the Italian people whilst Ludwig exercised his mind by engaging him in philosophical discussions. Amongst the occasional guests who found him sophisticated and charming were Sir Oswald Mosley, leader of the British League of Fascists, Sir Austen and Lady Chamberlain, the British Foreign Secretary and his wife, and Clementine Churchill, wife of the future wartime Prime Minister, Winston. In a letter to her husband, she described Mussolini as 'one of the most wonderful men in the world'!

If anything, his wife, who disliked city life in Rome or the company of her husband's friends, was even more reclusive. Until 1925, she lived with her children in Milan but moved to Carpena in Romagna before finally joining her husband in Rome in 1929. In spite of Mussolini's infidelities, she remained a tolerant wife who still regarded her husband with affection and because of this their marriage survived. During his early years Mussolini was involved in many affairs and had numerous mistresses. One, Ida Dalser, bore him a son and, once he was in power, she pestered him with claims that she was his legal wife. In 1926, she was arrested, certified insane and sent to a mental home where she died in 1937. In 1940, Mussolini began an affair with a Jewish woman, Margherita Sarfatti, who was an art critic working for *Avanti*. When race laws put her at risk, he saw to it that she moved to the safety of the United States. The true love of his life however was Claretta Petacci, the beautiful daughter of a highly respected Vatican physician. A former schoolgirl fan and 29 years his junior, her husband was discretely posted to Japan as an air attaché. Their relationship lasted during the war years and, as we shall see, in 1945, she chose to die with him.

The Mussolinis had five children. The eldest, Edda, was born in 1910, five years before her parents married. Somewhat unfairly described as 'fat and unshapely', she was certainly intelligent and vivacious and was to become her father's favourite. Amongst her early suitors was a Jewish boy but her father thought him unsuitable and she finally married Count Galeazzo Ciano, the son of an admiral and a loyal Fascist. Their marriage was the social event of 1930 and when her husband was appointed Italian envoy to China, they moved to Shanghai where their first child, Mussolini's first grandchild, was born. As we shall see, in 1943 Mussolini agreed to his son-in-law's arrest and execution, an act for which Edda never forgave her father.

A second son, Vittorio, was born in 1916. He was destined to become a film producer and worked on Fascist propaganda films but with no great success. During the Second World War, he served in the armed forces and afterwards made his way to Argentina. Bruno, who was born two years after his brother, became a pilot in the air force and saw action during the Italian invasion of Abyssinia. He was killed in 1941 when his aircraft crashed near Pisa during a test flight. In many ways, Romano, their third son might well be considered the most successful of the Mussolini brood. He became a fine jazz pianist and during his career toured Europe and America playing with many of the famous big bands and winning critical acclaim. During an early visit to Nazi Germany, he infuriated his guests when he played boogie-woogie that they considered American and decadent. A second daughter, Anna-Maria, was born to the Mussolinis in 1929 and in childhood was stricken with poliomyelitis. A strict father, Mussolini insisted that his children enjoyed no special privileges and they were all educated at state schools.

So much for Mussolini the man, now let us consider the other more dominating and threatening side of his character that was not always apparent to his family and friends. This was the image that his propagandists and those responsible for his public relations sought to create – a cult of personality, 'the cult of *Il Duce*'. Backed by the popular slogan, 'Mussolini is always right', he was presented to the Italian people as an infallible leader and world statesman who was working to restore the economy, saved them from Communism and restored their country's national prestige. Mussolini said, 'The crowd does not have to know, it must believe, it must submit to being shaped', and now regarded as a saviour, it was easy for him to influence public opinion and manipulate it. It was his obsession to ensure that Fascism permeated through all aspects of Italian life and the everyday lives of its citizens, it had to be reflected in business, industry, education, the judiciary, art, culture, sport, the armed services and, if possible, even religion. Not only were his image and the ideals of Fascism to be seen everywhere on posters, in newspapers and on the walls of public buildings, in addition subtle use was made of slogans such as 'Mussolini is God', 'Believe! Obey! Fight!' and the more profound 'Better one day as a lion than a hundred years as a sheep.' Newspaper editors were instructed to expand and embroider the achievements of Fascism and play down or not mention at all its failures. Since Mussolini disliked references to death, obituaries were no longer published in the press and there was no popular call to celebrate his fiftieth birthday. In order to prove that *Il Duce* was no ordinary man, Fascist propagandists portrayed him as energetic, virile and assertive – a superman-type figure. Pictures were circulated that showed him stripped to the waist driving a tractor at harvest time whilst others portrayed him as a daredevil racing driver of cars and motorcycles, fearless aviator, skilled horseman, master skier, swashbuckling swordsman, and virtuoso violinist. Ironically, he was accomplished in many of these skills though not to the degree his propagandists claimed. As you can imagine, abroad and amongst his opponents at home, this style of propaganda attracted a great deal of ridicule.

There was, however, one talent that Mussolini unquestionably possessed, the gift of spellbinding oratory. He was not just simply a ranting rabble-rouser, but a skilled motivator and his speeches were vigorous and delivered staccato style. He tended to begin quietly but as he progressed, so he became increasingly agitated so his voice rose to a crescendo as his eyes rolled and he used his hands to make wild gesticulations. When he paused, he would stand akimbo with hands on hips and chin jutting forward to give his ecstatic crowd time to applaud. Later, at home, he would watch his performance on film, gauge its effect on his audience and consider improvements in his style and delivery. In the presence of photographers, he invariably refused to smile but instead maintained a facial expression that was half scowl and half pout. Always oozing self-confidence, he once said, 'I would often like to be wrong, but it never happens.' It is certainly true that Mussolini spent more time on speech making and self-promotion than he did on either Party matters or formulating policy.

Like many politicians of today, Mussolini liked to appear in public with celebrities. In 1933, he was frequently seen in public with Primo Carnera, the so-called 'Ambling Alp', the Italian who had won the world heavy-weight boxing title. The association was quickly dropped when a year later Carnera lost his title to the American, Max Baer. Later, when Carnera expressed anti-Fascist sympathies, he was sent to a labour camp! *Il Duce* also liked to be seen in the company of the world famous Italian conductor, Arturo Toscanini until the maestro protested against new racial laws and left to make his home in the United States. However, Mussolini had better luck with the famous tenor Beniamo Gigli, whom he referred to as 'the people's singer of Italy' and the inventor, Gugliemo Marconi. Marconi joined the Party in 1923 and later became a member of the Fascist Grand Council.

Mussolini was also given to gross exaggeration and once claimed that he could mobilize '8 million bayonets and manufacture sufficient aircraft to blot out the sky' when he well knew that no such armaments existed. Many historians feel that his bombast, flamboyance and self-promotion were nothing more than a façade intended to cover his insecurity. The American historian, T. Koon, expressed the view that 'Mussolini's greatest talent, perhaps his only talent, was his ability to manufacture myths and slogans that captured the public imagination.' The problem was that as the Mussolini myth grew, he came to believe it himself and as he found it increasingly difficult to distinguish between what was true and false and what was relevant and what was superfluous, so he became divorced from reality. But then, to what extent did the Italian people fall for his sloganeering and propaganda? If we can accept the election results of 1929 as accurate when 8,506,576 Italians voted for the Fascists and only a paltry 136,198 against, then it would appear that the vast majority had succumbed, but did the result truly reflect the views of the people?

Leading figures in the Fascist hierarchy

At first, Mussolini rewarded his stalwart supporters in the Fascist leadership with appointments to the government or ambassadorships and governorships of overseas colonies. These acts of patronage did not however ensure their long term loyalty and, as we shall see, during the Second World War when things began to go badly wrong, several turned against their leader and those that failed to escape abroad were arrested and executed. First amongst the hierarchy were the four who had formed the quadrumvirate at the time of the Fascist march on Rome, Italo Balbo, Michele Bianchi, Emilo De Bono and Cesare De Vecchi. Bianchi was one of Mussolini's closest supporters who served in turn as Party Secretary, Under-Secretary of the Interior and Minister of Public Works but his early death in 1930 robbed his leader of one of his most reliable friends and close associates. One of the more flamboyant of the Fascist hierarchy, Italo Balbo, served Mussolini as Minister of Aviation and was responsible for the development of aviation in Italy. In 1933, he was appointed Governor-General of Libya and there worked to win Islamic support for Fascism. However, in 1938 he blotted his copybook when he spoke out against Italy's alliance with Germany and afterwards Mussolini never truly trusted him. Emilo De Bono served as Colonial Secretary and, as we shall see, commanded the Italian armies that invaded Abyssinia in 1935. In 1943, he voted against Mussolini in the Fascist Grand Council and was summarily tried and executed. His leader rewarded Cesare De Vecchi by in turn appointing him Governor of Somalia, ambassador to the Vatican and briefly Minister of Education. However, like De Bono he voted against Mussolini in 1943 and was fortunate to be sentenced to death in his absence. Another who eventually suffered the same fate was Dino Grandi. In 1929, Grandi was appointed Mussolini's Foreign Minister and afterwards served as Italian ambassador in London and finally as Minister of Justice. He too joined the revolt against his leader in 1943 and was sentenced to death but managed to escape to Portugal. On the extreme right of the Party was the unpopular Roberto Farinacci who was disliked by Mussolini and most of the other members of the Fascist hierarchy. He became Party Secretary in 1935 and edited the newspaper, *Regime Fascista*. Unlike the others, he was racialist and strongly anti-Semitic and was later responsible for the persecution of Italian Jews. An admirer of Hitler, he played a

leading role in establishing Italy's close relationship with
Germany. Towards the end of the war, he was captured by
Italian partisans and shot. A career soldier with the additional
title of Marquess of Neghelli, Rodolfo Graziani served in the
First World War and in 1935 was appointed Governor of
Somaliland. As we shall see, following the conquest of Abyssinia
he became the ruthless Viceroy of Ethiopia and commanded the
Italian armies in North Africa during the Second World War.
After his failures, he became Minister of Defence and led the
armed resistance against the Allied invasion of his country in
1944. After the war, the Allies put him on trial and he was
sentenced to a term of imprisonment but, since he was now in
his mid-seventies, he was granted an early release.

Mussolini gains control of the Party and parliament

By 1926, Mussolini had taken steps such as the Acerbo Law to
ensure that the Fascist Party dominated Italian politics and he
was in a position to ignore parliament and rule by decree.
However, this was not sufficient since his ultimate aim was to
concentrate all power in his own hands and establish a one-
man, totalitarian dictatorship and this meant taking control of
the Fascist Party as well as parliament.

To exercise total control of the Party would not be easy since
whilst local leaders, the *ras,* usually paid him lip service but
were not always prepared to go along with and implement his
policy decisions. The *ras* represented the more radical right-
wing views of the Party and Mussolini would need to use
considerable subtlety in dealing with them. Since the *squadristi*
had been the cornerstone of the authority of the *ras*, his decision
to turn them into a disciplined militia was a shrewd move since
this placed them under his control. His next step was to purge
the Party of dissidents and members whose loyalty was suspect.
Within the Party, there were those with different self-interests –
the nationalist, socialist and conservative elements – and
Mussolini cunningly played one group off against the others so
that their differences gradually became muted and finally lapsed
altogether. In the end, the Party surrendered to Mussolini with
surprising ease and in order to secure his position even further,
he made sure that senior positions in the Party were held by men
who presented no threat to him and that the Party Secretary was
a man of undisputed loyalty.

As we have seen, by 1925 Mussolini had banned all the opposition parties and after passing the Acerbo Law was able to rule by decree. In fact, parliament had become defunct and there was no real need for it to meet at all since Mussolini's policy decisions invariably gained approval sometimes even without the formality of a vote.

Of course, there were other institutions in Italy that needed to be brought into line – local government, the civil service, the judiciary and the armed forces. To gain control of them, Mussolini used stealth and, as we have seen in local government, he simply removed people likely to be difficult and replaced them with by Party appointees. As far as those employed in the civil service were concerned, they soon discovered that membership of the Fascist Party was essential for promotion and by 1935, Party membership had become a condition of employment. In the judiciary, judges, barristers and solicitors who lacked enthusiasm for Fascism were declared undesirable and removed. There were also occasions when Mussolini directly intervened in trials and decided verdicts and punishments. Since the military leaders largely shared Mussolini's foreign policy ambitions, gaining control of the armed forces proved relatively easy. Already Italian servicemen wore Fascist insignia on their uniforms and gave the raised arm Fascist salute and Mussolini impressed senior officers by seeing to it that recruitment was increased and that more was spent on the production and development of modern weapons.

The effect of Mussolini's domination of all the major national institutions was a substantial increase in the number of technocrats and civil service administrators and this was reflected in the make-up of the Party. Whilst white-collar worker representation in the Party increased considerably so the membership of workers and peasants fell dramatically. Even worse and in spite of the increase in numbers, the confusion in the administration worsened, officials became notorious for accepting bribes. Promotion, the award of contracts and the granting of favours became dependent on having the right contacts or knowing someone prepared to accept a bribe or *bustarella*. The Italians applied the term *bustarella* to the brown envelope known to contain a back-hander or bribe.

The suffrage was further narrowed and many of the working class lost the vote when changes in the electoral system were introduced in 1928 that limited the vote to men over 21 who were members of syndicates, that is Fascist-style trade unions, or paid substantial sums in taxes. Consequently, the electorate fell from 10 to 3 million.

Il Duce and King Victor Emmanuel III

Victor Emmanuel III became King following the assassination of his father, Umberto I, in 1900. Small in stature and noted for his untidy appearance, he was nicknamed 'the dwarf'. A shy and reclusive man he soon became the cartoonists' delight as they portrayed him in a series of cruel caricatures. He had supported Italy's entry into the war in 1915 and, even after the debacle of Caporetto, continued to vigorously support his country's participation in the conflict. His conduct after the war proved highly controversial and to a degree it can be claimed that he was responsible for Mussolini's successful rise to power and survival in office. You will recall that in 1922 he refused to call on the army to disperse the Fascist march on Rome and instead offered him the premiership. Again in 1924, he declined to be part of any move to oust Mussolini at the time of the Matteotti crisis and afterwards did nothing to prevent the Fascist leader infringing the Italian Constitution which, on his accession, he had sworn to uphold.

Although in public, the two men put on a pretence of friendship, in truth the relations between the two men was always tense. The King appreciated that he needed Mussolini's support to retain the throne whilst *Il Duce* knew that any move to remove Victor Emmanuel might offend conservatives, monarchists and the military. The two men met twice weekly and on each occasion the monarch dutifully signed any decree placed before him. However, there were some occasions when they disagreed. The King did not approve of the inclusion of the Fascist emblem on the national flag or the powers granted to the Fascist Grand Council but he did not openly oppose either. Mussolini and Victor Emmanuel seldom appeared in public together and, in private, there was no love lost between them. Although the King thought his Prime Minister 'vulgar and offensive', he was afraid of him and it was fear of offending him that caused him to decline to attend the funeral of Giovanni Giolitti in 1928. By 1930, the King had surrendered all his responsibilities and to all intents and purposes the Italian monarchy had become an irrelevance.

Years of repression

By 1928, it might have appeared that there was little point and some considerable risk in opposing Mussolini. Even so, there remained some with sufficient courage to continue to defy the regime. Across the country, Communists formed underground cells and published and circulated their own clandestine newspaper, *Unita* (Unity), and distributed anti-Fascist leaflets. Another group, *Giustizia e Liberta*, Justice and Liberty, was led by Carlo Roselli. Their aim was to bring about an alliance between Italian Socialists and Liberals. Imprisoned by the authorities, Roselli escaped and managed to reach France where he made the world's press aware of the atrocities being carried out by the Fascist regime. Later, during the Spanish Civil War (1936–9), he supported the left-wing Republicans and fought with the International Brigade. During this time, he famously used the slogan 'Today Spain; tomorrow Italy'. In 1937, Roselli and his brother were murdered on the French Riviera by the *Cagoulards*, a group of French Fascists.

In Italy, opponents of Mussolini's Fascists constantly faced the terror of the murderous *squadristi* who murdered some 2,000 victims and tortured, wounded and maimed thousands more. In pretence of using more legitimate ways to curb opponents, Mussolini increased the number of civilian police, the *polizia*, and, as we have seen, turned the squadristi into an official uniformed militia. Led by Arturo Bocchini, who was known to have a gigantic appetite for both food and women and treated police funds as his own, the force of 50,000 men used terms taken from Roman times. Individual units were known as legions and certain officers held the rank of centurions. In 1926, Zamboni's attempt to assassinate Mussolini (see page 74) led to the creation of a new, secret police force of state repression, the *Organizzazione Vigilanza Repressione Antifascismo,* the OVRA. A new tribunal, the *Tribuna Speciale Per La Difesa Dello Stato,* was set up to deal with those identified as being a danger to public safety. These were defined as:

> Those who have committed or have shown any intention of committing any act intended to disturb the national, social or economic functions of the State...or to impede the carrying out of the functions of the State in such a manner as to injure in any way the national interests either at home or abroad.

Such people were removed from their homes and made liable to detention in a 'compulsory domicile' for between one and five years in a colony or commune. The powers of the OVRA were extended to allow them to hold suspects without trial, carry out searches, tap telephones and intercept mail. They also committed acts of violence although members of the general public who were not politically active or hostile to Fascism were usually left alone. Clearly, the purpose of the OVRA was to impress on the Italian people the need to conform and the risks involved of doing otherwise.

Between 1927 and 1943, the *Tribuna* sat on 720 occasions and considered 13,547 cases. Of these 5,155 were found guilty and only 49 sentenced to death. Prison sentences varied in length, other punishments included being held under house arrest or *confino*. *Confino* meant being banished to a penal colony where, by all accounts, conditions were far from severe and not worked to death like the inmates of Stalin's labour camps or subjected to the cruelties of Hitler's concentration camps. Apart from attending roll-calls, they could mainly do as they wished, were paid five lire a day and were entitled to compassionate leave.

Latterly, the Fascist campaign against Freemasonry intensified until Freemason orders were finally abolished. They also turned upon the long established illegal brotherhood of criminals, the *Mafia*. Their leaders were arrested and brought to trial and the illegal activities of this notorious criminal element in Italian society brought to an end. The Fascists also took measures to 'Italianize' the German, Austrian and Slav minorities who, as a result of the Treaty of St Germain, lived in their newly acquired border regions. It was not until 1938 and at Hitler's instigation that Mussolini finally turned against the Jews.

Mussolini's regime – its strengths and weaknesses

As is usual, the popular appeal of any government lies firstly in its promises and then in its ability to keep those promises. Mussolini promised the Italian people political stability, economic prosperity and the restoration of Italy's national prestige and although he went some way towards achieving some of these, we shall see later that gradually early enthusiasm of the people gave way to disillusionment.

A trump card played by Mussolini was to cash in on the fear of some sections of the community – industrialists, businessmen, landowners and the upper and middle classes – of Communism. His propagandists were also able to use his oratory and personal charisma to good effect in winning over the masses and by eliminating in turn the Italian parliament, the Grand Council, the *ras* and the trade unions, Mussolini was able to create a one-man dictatorship. Whilst censorship of the press and other media made it difficult for opposed views to be heard, he could also depend on the Fascist militia (MVSN) and the OVRA to eliminate the first sign of unease or disagreement. Later, he took measures to win over the support of many Roman Catholics and Fascist indoctrination of the young went some way to ensuring the future continued support for Fascism.

However, was Mussolini's hold on the Italian people really as firm as it may seem? His lack of clear-cut policies and his failure to achieve their ends might easily lead to disillusionment and despite his efforts to eradicate them, opponents to his regime remained active. As the activities of the MVSN and OVRA became less brutal for how long would they be able to intimidate the people? There were still instances when public opinion might be outraged as was evident at the time of the murder of Matteotti. Since some already thought his antics absurd, how long would it be before the Italian people saw through Mussolini's posturing and self-promotion as a cult figure? The regime's attempt to censor the press and other media were far from effective and many parents objected to the indoctrination of their children. The truth was that for as long as the realization of Mussolini's promises of a better future seemed possible, the bulk of the Italian people would tolerate his methods but what would happen when his achievements failed to match his rhetoric and things began to go wrong?

08 life in Fascist Italy

This chapter will cover:
- the relations between the Fascist State and the Roman Catholic Church
- the Fascist education system and youth movements
- the role of women in Fascist Italy
- the extent of Fascist intrusion into the everyday lives of the people
- Fascist art and culture
- the coming of racism and anti-Semitism.

'Women should be exemplary wives and mothers, guardians of the hearth, and subject to the legitimate authority of their husbands.'
(Mussolini's view of the role of women in Fascist society.)

The Fascist State and the Roman Catholic Church

Since the majority of Italians were Roman Catholics, it was important to Mussolini that, in order that he retained the support of the Italian people, he should end the on-going rift between the State and the Catholic Church. It was important too since it would enhance his reputation both at home and abroad. The problem dated back to 1870 when Pope Pius IX refused to recognize the new united Kingdom of Italy. Earlier in his life, Mussolini declared himself an atheist and had been a fierce and outspoken critic of Roman Catholicism. He had poured scorn on the Church's rites and teachings and had written a pamphlet, *God Does Not Exist* whilst his book, *The Cardinal's Mistress*, proved offensive to Catholics and he was dubbed 'the enemy of true faith'. More recently, Fascist extremists had attacked churches and interrupted religious processions. Although on the face of it, the Fascist regime and the Catholic Church appeared to co-exist harmoniously, Mussolini felt that it was time for him appease the Papal authorities and reach a formal agreement acceptable to both sides.

In 1923, during his maiden speech to the Chamber of Deputies, Mussolini made favourable references to the Church and for their part, the Church authorities applauded his anti-Socialist measures, his opposition to atheistic Communism and his decision to outlaw Freemasonry. Mussolini next saw to it that the Catholic ritual was restored to public ceremonies and the symbol of the crucifix reappeared in schools and the law courts. Religious instruction once again appeared in the curriculum of schools and Milan's Catholic university was given official recognition. In addition, the state allowances to Catholic priests were increased and they were exempt from taxation. Mussolini next appeared as the champion of family values when the laws relating to divorce were tightened, penalties introduced for adultery, contraception frowned upon and abortion made almost impossible. *Il Duce*'s new standards of morality went even further when swearing in public and infection by syphilis were declared offences and gambling and heavy drinking discouraged. For Italian women, the wearing of short skirts and heavy make-up were discouraged and dancing deemed to be immoral and improper. As a personal gesture, in 1925 Mussolini and his wife, Rachele, ten years after their civil ceremony went through a religious wedding service and had their children baptized. Little wonder that some Catholic priests spoke favourably of Fascism and agreed to bless Fascist regalia and banners. However, in spite of these concessions, the conflict between Church and State remained since Mussolini refused to restore to the Pope the former Papal States and any solution could only possibly be reached through a compromise.

Eventually, with Cardinal Pietro Gasparri representing the papacy, negotiations began in an atmosphere of suspicion and mutual distrust. Progress was painfully slow and extended over three years of hard bargaining. During this time, Mussolini let it be known that if no agreement was reached, he would begin a campaign of violence against the Church and so, not surprisingly, in February 1929, the Lateran Treaty was finally signed.

The Lateran Treaty of 1929

The final agreement consisted of two documents, a treaty and a concordat. The treaty, which covered the territorial and financial arrangements, recognized papal sovereignty over 44 hectares in the centre of Rome around St Peter's. Known as the Vatican City, it was to be allowed to have its own diplomatic corps, army, police and courts, radio station, newspaper and postal services. In return, the Pope finally recognized the Kingdom of Italy with Rome as its capital city. In return for giving up its claim to the former Papal States, the Church was to receive 750 million lire in money and a further 1,000 million lire in government bonds. The Concordat was intended to regulate the relations between the Church and the State. Under its terms, Roman Catholicism was recognized as the official or established religion of the State of Italy although the State maintained the right to veto Church appointments and Catholic clergy agreed to be uninvolved in politics. Civil marriage was no longer a requirement and divorce became impossible without the sanction of the Church. Finally, religious teaching was to become compulsory in all state primary and secondary schools.

Who then got the best deal? Certainly some Fascists thought that Mussolini had gone too far and given away more than was necessary. Mussolini did not see it that way, he had won the blessing of the Catholic Church and the people were delighted and praised him as the man who had 'given back God to Italy and Italy to God'. Further, *Il Duce* did not consider the Lateran Treaty to be an agreement between equals but an alliance between Church and State that left the Catholic Church subordinate to the State. The terms also showed that he was no longer prepared to tolerate papal criticism of Fascist policies and that he was determined to exclude the Church from Italian politics. It was inevitable that old differences would soon re-emerge and this was evident when on his first visit to the Vatican, Mussolini made a point of refusing to kiss the Pope's hand. Even more serious was the crisis that developed over Catholic Action.

Catholic Action dated back to 1865 when it was established to be responsible for the organization and management of Catholic youth groups. Under Fascism, the Catholic Boy Scout movement was the only remaining body actively engaged in caring for the interests of young Catholics. Although Article 43 of the Concordat recognized its independence, Mussolini felt that its activities encroached on those of Fascist youth movements and he decided to disband it. Afterwards, there was criticism of Catholic Action in the press and attacks on its premises and members. However, Pope Pius XI was not an easy man to browbeat and in 1931 he responded with the encyclical *Non Abiamo Bisogno* – 'We have no need.' In his circular letter to his bishops he wrote:

> We have protested against the campaign of false and unjust accusations that preceded the disbanding of the associations of young people and of university students affiliated with Catholic Action. It is wrong for Fascists to monopolise completely the young from the tenderest years up to manhood and womanhood, all for the exclusive advantage of the Party, of a regime based on ideology which clearly resolves itself into a true and real pagan worship of the State…The idea of the State which makes young generations belong entirely to it…cannot be reconciled by a Catholic with Catholic doctrine and Catholic practice…

The publication of the encyclical immediately caused a rumpus and in Italy its publication was banned. However, the eminent American Cardinal, Francis Spellman, saw to it that copies reached France and it was also published in the papal newspaper, *L'Osservatore Romano*. Copies were smuggled out of the Vatican and it was widely read by the Italian public. In the end, a disgruntled Mussolini had to agree to a compromise by which Catholic Action was allowed to continue provided it did not appoint officials known to belong to 'groups adverse to the regime'. It also had to agree that its members concentrated only on educational and recreational activities and did not become involved in sporting activities. This was clearly a move intended to prevent Catholic Action from engaging in activities that brought it into direct competition with Fascist youth organizations. Afterwards there was a period of relative harmony between the Church and the Fascist regime but, as we shall see, this was to end once Mussolini began the persecution of Italy's Jews.

Indoctrination – the Fascist education system and youth movements

In Hitler's Germany, Stalin's Russia and all totalitarian states, the indoctrination of the young was essential since it was supposed to guarantee that future generations would remain loyal and unquestioningly continue to support the regime and its ideology. In this respect, Mussolini's Italy was no different. In Italy, education was provided by state schools and a range of independent schools, the majority of which were Catholic. The aim of the Fascist education system was not merely to produce committed and unwavering young Fascists but also to mould the characters of children and so create mentally and physically perfect 'new men and women'. However, before such grandiose aims could be achieved, Italy had first to deal with the problem of illiteracy in order to produce a new generation of highly qualified men and women needed as the country moved forward into a more advanced technological age. The task of laying down the guidelines for the future was given to the university professor and educationalist Giovanni Gentile and he was also intended to oversee the publication of the *Enciclopedia Italiana*, a work of scholarship not unlike the *Encyclopedia Britannica*. His plan was to provide improved facilities for the most able children so that they could attain standards of excellence. The less gifted were to receive 'more suitable and relevant education'. His policies were seen as class structured and not well received by some Fascists and Gentile's influence diminished as Mussolini became increasingly involved in framing education policy.

His successors were to follow very different principles with the school curriculum revised in order to accommodate Fascist ideology. In all classrooms, a portrait of Mussolini hung beside that of Victor Emmanuel III as well as posters illustrating Fascist attitudes and achievements. Teachers were expected to emphasize Mussolini's genius and each day began and ended with the chanting of Fascist slogans such as *Mussolini ha sempre ragione* (Mussolini is always right). In order to conform to Fascist ideology, all textbooks had to be rewritten and one government-sponsored textbook introduced into junior schools, the *libro unico*, covered all subjects. Children were taught that Italy was 'the true cradle of European civilisation' and much of the teaching concentrated on Italian history and literature. As far as history was concerned, teachers concentrated on the greatness of the Roman Empire, the Italian Renaissance, the struggle to achieve unification – Italian unification – the *Risorgimento* and of course, the rise of Mussolini and Fascism. In textbooks, the truth was also hidden with claims such as that it was Italy's entry into the First World War that decided the outcome and that Italians alone won the Battle of Vittorio Veneto!

Schools were all single-sex and great emphasis was placed on physical fitness and out-of-door activities and in accordance with the terms of the Lateran Treaty, religious education was taught in all schools. The highest profile was given to Fascist indoctrination with young children taught to read and write by using books that contained Fascist-type cartoons and quotations from Mussolini's speeches. At the end of the day they chanted *Credere! Obbedire! Combattere!* – 'Believe! Obey! Fight!' They were also warned, 'The eyes of the Duce are on every one of you' and a child who dared to ask 'why?' was told, 'You obey because you must.'

In 1938, the authorities published a Fascist Decalogue for use in secondary schools that was really a crude and distorted version of the Ten Commandments. It read:

1 Remember that those who fell for the revolution and for the empire march at the head of your columns.

2 Your comrade is your brother. He lives with you, thinks with you, and is at your side in battle.

3 Service to Italy can be given at all times, in all places and by every means. It can be paid with toil and also with blood.

4 The enemy of Fascism is your enemy. Show him no mercy.

5 Discipline is the sunshine of armies. It prepares and illuminates the victory.

6 He who advances to attack with determination has victory already in his grasp.

7 Conscious and complete obedience is the virtue of the soldier.

8 There do not exist important and unimportant things. There is only duty.

9 The Fascist revolution has depended on the past and still depends on the bayonets of its soldiers.

10 Mussolini is always right.

In 1939, a Fascist School Charter was put forward by Giueseppe Bottai who considered the old education system to be too bourgeois. The aim of the new Charter was to promote 'the eternal value of the Italian race and civilisation' and it was intended to concentrate more on the needs of the less able, non-academic pupils. Schools were now to be classified as elementary, intermediate and superior. After attending nursery schools, *Scoula Materna*, children proceeded to elementary schools where they stayed until the age of 14. This was followed by five years at an intermediate school before going on to superior lyceums and institutes. Promotion from one stage to the next was determined by examination and not by age and the State provided all textbooks and other educational materials. In 1943, Bottai quarrelled with Mussolini and using the name André Bataille escaped from Italy to join the French Foreign Legion and fight against the Germans!

Teachers who could not be reconciled to Fascism were dismissed. In 1931 all teachers had to swear an oath of loyalty in which they undertook to be loyal to the Fascist regime and carry out their duties with the aim of training children to be 'upright and hardworking citizens who are devoted to the fatherland and to the Fascist regime'. In the same year, all teachers' associations were merged into a Fascist Association and two years later, all teachers had to be members of the Fascist Party and wear Fascist uniforms on special occasions. It is impossible to assess how successful the Fascists were in trying to indoctrinate their young. They had obstacles to overcome – the Church, unconvinced teachers who joined the Party merely to retain their teaching posts and parents who objected to having their children brain-washed. In fairness it should be noted that with increased government expenditure on education and the raising of the school leaving age, the illiteracy rate fell rapidly.

As students had already been subjected to years of Fascist indoctrination in the elementary and secondary schools, there was little need to continue with the process at university. Anyway, by this time, the battle to win over the minds of intelligent and more mature students had already been won or lost. Nevertheless, university students were expected to join the *Gioventi Unniversitaria Fascista*, the University Fascist Youth and the majority did so because of the advantages of membership – enhanced career prospects and future military service. Unlike school teachers, university lecturers could not be so easily replaced. Many had to be coaxed to join the Party and take the oath of allegiance but did so because they were told they were mere formalities. Again there were positive aspects since during the Fascist period the number of students at Italian universities rose from 54,000 in 1921 to 165,000 in 1942. Furthermore, students came from more diverse backgrounds than had previously been the case.

Fascist youth movements

The indoctrination of Italian children continued after the end of the school day, at weekends and during the holidays and this was achieved through membership of youth organizations that made up the *Opera Nazionale Balilla*, the ONB or just simply the *Balilla*. The movement, that took its name from Giovan Battista Perasso, nicknamed Balilla, a youth who had played a part in the uprising against the Austrians in 1756, was divided into a number of different units each of which catered for a different age group. At the age of six, boys and girls joined the *Figli Della Lupa*, the 'Children of the She-Wolf' and at the age of eight boys transferred to the *Balilla* and girls to the *Piccole Italiane*. Girls moved on to the *Giovani Italiane* at the age of 13 whilst 15-year-old boys became members of the *Avanguardisti*. Apart from continuing the process of indoctrination, membership of the various sections of the youth movement made available a wide range of activities and this meant that many joined in order to take advantage of the facilities rather than out of political conviction. Sports and physical exercise were encouraged as was attendance at weekend rallies and summer camps. Much attention was also given to the militaristic aspects of the movement and uniformed boy members were expected to take part in arms drills with miniature rifles and bayonets and attend parades, whilst girls enjoyed more feminine pursuits and received instruction in cookery and childcare. Of course, the *Balilla* had to contend with the counter attractions offered by the youth organizations run by the Catholic Church and as members got older so their enthusiasm waned and their attendance lapsed. Not too surprisingly, the motto of the youth organizations was *Credere! Obbedire! Combattere!* And members had to swear an oath of loyalty to Mussolini and learn by heart the *Balilla* Creed which was a crude and not too original version of the Apostles' Creed:

> I believe in Rome the Eternal, the mother of my country, and in Italy her eldest daughter, who was born of the virginal bosom by the grace of God; who suffered through the barbarian invasions, was crucified and buried; who descended to the grave and was raised from the dead in the nineteenth century, who ascended into Heaven in her glory in 1918 and 1922, who is seated on the right hand of her mother Rome; who for this reason shall come to judge the living and the dead. I believe in the genius of Mussolini, in our Holy Father, Fascism, in the communion of its martyrs, in the conversion of Italians, and the resurrection of the Empire.

Members of the *Balilla* wore black shirts, the *camica nera,* grey short trousers, blue scarves and black tasseled hats whilst the uniforms of the older *Avanguardisti* resembled those of adult Blackshirts. At meetings, members joined together to sing the Fascist hymn, the *Giovinezza*, or Youth. To start with, the leader of the Fascist youth movement was Renato Ricci but in 1937, he quarrelled with the Party Secretary, Achille Starace, who removed him. Afterwards the *Opera Nazionale Balilla* became part of the Party controlled *Gioventu Italiana Del Littorioa,* GIL or Young Fascists of the Lictor. A lictor was the official who, in Roman times, went before a magistrate carrying the fasces. Once membership of the GIL was made compulsory, joining became automatic and therefore to many, a meaningless gesture. Even so, the membership rose to an impressive 8.5 million.

The role of women in Fascist society

So far, we have only considered women that were associated with Mussolini – his mother, Rosa, his wife, Rachele, his daughters, Edda and Anna, and his string of mistresses. As we have seen, Fascist Italy was very much male dominated and so women had a strictly defined role. In his speeches, Mussolini did not mince words – 'Child bearing is woman's natural and fundamental role in life' and 'Women should be exemplary wives and mothers, guardians of the hearth, and subject to the legitimate authority of their husbands.' In other words, a woman's role was simply child bearing and running the home and consequently there seemed little point in women being given access to further education. Although women were not actually banned from colleges and universities and even though they were not encouraged, some did gain advanced qualifications but then found that there were few job opportunities and promotion to prestigious positions was virtually unheard of. Of course, women were still employed in such traditional work as teaching and nursing and some became telephonists or accepted more menial work as waitresses and cleaners. Although the number was limited by a quota system, an increasing number of women were employed in factories whilst in the countryside, the employment of women on the land, particularly at times of planting and harvesting, was essential to the rural economy. Whatever their employment, it did not exclude them from their childbearing role.

The Fascists were on the prudish side regarding the appearance of their womenfolk. They were to wear simple, plain clothes and avoid revealing dresses, high-heeled shoes and cosmetics. The ideal woman was considered to be amply built and matronly. Of course, many Italian women went to the cinema where they caught glimpses of beautifully clothed Hollywood actresses and scantily dressed females at athletic events. Mussolini was against women becoming involved in sports since it was believed that it might cause infertility. Although neither he nor his family adhered to the norm, *Il Duce* expressed the view that a family of 12 was ideal. In a country where widowhood at any age brought with it the necessity to wear black, the overall appearance of Italian women would have been drab in the extreme. In spite of this, the wives of leading Fascist officials and professional men continued to buy their clothes from leading Paris fashion houses and enjoy French perfumes. Is it perhaps ironic that this period witnessed the birth of two women destined to be amongst Italy's most celebrated beauties – Gina Lollobrigida, born in 1927, and Sophia Loren, born in 1934?

Although the vote was extended to women in 1925, it was only for use in local government elections and they remained excluded from politics. There were a small number of women-only sections of the Fascist Party and the best known of these was the *Fasci Femminili* that became divided into the *Sezione Massaie* for peasant women and the *Sezione Operaie e Lavoranti a Domicilio* for working class women. Women could also join the *Opera Nazionale per la Maternita Ed Infanzia* that was set up to care for housewives and mothers in need. The additional care provided ensured that the number of still births fell and there was an overall decline in the infant mortality rate. Unfortunately, these organizations had little or no influence on population growth and in 1927, Mussolini embarked on a Battle for Births.

The Battle for Births

Mussolini, who was convinced that his country needed to have an increasing and predominantly young population to supply the needs of the army, industry and populate Italy's overseas empire, was alarmed by the continuing fall in the Italian birth rate. In order to reverse the trend, in 1927 the Fascist leader launched a Battle for Births with the aim of increasing the population of Italy, which was then 40 million, to 60 million by 1950. To achieve this, he put forward a policy that would include generous rewards for those that married and contributed to the growth of the population and penalties for those who remained single. The Battle was backed by a propaganda campaign that suggested that a family of 12 children was ideal and loans were offered to couples when they married with part of it subsequently cancelled with every child born. The loan was considered to have been repaid with the birth of the sixth child. Each year in the Palazzo Venezia, Mussolini personally presented additional rewards and medals to the mothers of the largest families. Those who remained unmarried were punished for their celibacy by being forced to pay higher levels of taxation and having their promotion blocked. In 1933, the number of women employed in the public sector was subject to a quota of 10 per cent of the total workforce and this was later applied to firms in the private sector. The quota system was not applied to women employed in low paid, menial occupations. An article in a British newspaper described the situation:

> The decline in births in Italy leads to the conclusion that in the event of mobilisation there would be a shortage of 600,000 soldiers. The Fascist revolution will do its best to fill this gap. You must get married and have children, a lot of children. There are inducements – the citizens who have at least six children are exempt from all taxation...The bachelor is hit by a special tax, which is highest, for those aged thirty-five to fifty. That is not all. He is also handicapped in his career. A married man is always

preferred to a bachelor...Once married, he is entitled to help with special payments, the first of which is the cost of the honeymoon railway journey. To Rome, of course.

(From an article in *The Times* in December 1934.)

It was convenient that much of the concept of the Battle for Births coincided with Catholic doctrine and was subsequently supported by the Church. Yet in spite of the system of rewards and punishments, there was no increase in the number of marriages and the birth rate marginally declined.

table 7 Italian birth and death rates 1900–50			
	Number of births per thousand of the population	Number of deaths per thousand of the population	Total population (millions)
1900	33.0	23.8	37
1920	32.3	19.0	40
1930	26.7	14.1	45
1940	23.5	13.6	47.5

(Source: International Historical Statistics, Europe 1750–1988 by B. R. Mitchell, Government Publication, 1992.)

Fascist intrusion into the everyday lives of the people

From what we have already read, we can see that Fascism impinged considerably on the everyday lives of the Italian people. They were banned from belonging to opposition political parties and trade unions, their press, radio, films and theatrical productions were censored and they were bombarded with a torrent of propaganda. They were powerless to prevent the indoctrination of their children and women were largely denied the benefits of higher education, their job opportunities were limited and they were encouraged to marry and devote their lives to the home and raising large families. In addition, the regime tried to impose acceptable styles of clothes and a code of conduct on young women. Young men were liable for national service and in many of their chosen occupations found promotion impossible unless they were members of the Party. On top of all this, they had to tolerate the uniform wearing, flag waving, drum beating and slogan chanting that was part of the razzmatazz of Fascist pageantry. As we have seen, upper class

Italians were less affected by Fascist intervention than others. Their wives still bought French clothes and perfumes, they still carried on with their high life and party-going and enjoyed foreign holidays. In fairness too, not all Fascist intrusion was undesirable since it included the introduction of a series of welfare measures – the provision of sickness and unemployment benefits, the payment of family allowances and help for poorer families during the winter months. The man most responsible for imposing Fascist standards on the people was the Party Secretary, Achille Starace.

Starace, a qualified accountant who had served in the First World War, came from a well-to-do family and after joining the Fascist Party, promotion came quickly. Described by the historian Denis Mack Smith as 'unintelligent, humourless, utterly obedient and an unctuous flatterer', he had a police record for involvement in vice, drugs, rape and embezzlement and must be ranked as one of the most thoroughly unpleasant of all the Fascist leaders. In 1931, he replaced Augusto Turati as Party Secretary after falsely accusing him of sado-masochism, incest and paedophelia. As Party Secretary, he worked to achieve two aims – to promote even further Mussolini's cult of personality and introduce Fascist uniformity into every aspect of the everyday life of the Italian people. It was he who insisted that Fascists greeted each other with the raised arm salute and conclude their letters with *Viva Il Duce*. Starace is also credited with coining the slogan '*Credere! Obbediere! Combattere!*' and insisted that people should stand and salute at the mere mention of *Il Duce*'s name. His loyalty to Mussolini was total and he hardly deserved his leader's estimate of him as 'being a cretin but an obedient one'.

One of the most impressive Fascist achievements of this period was the attempt to provide the people with improved leisure facilities through the *Opera Nazionale Dopolavoro*, ONP.

The *Opera Nazionale Dopolavoro*

The *Opera Nazionale Dopolavoro*, the National Institution for Leisure Activities, usually referred to as simply, *Dopolavoro*, was just another attempt by Starace to influence the masses this time by intruding into their free time. Its stated aims were to provide healthy and profitable leisure time activities and improve the quality of life of the Italian people. Starace himself summed up the aims of *Dolopavoro*:

To loosen the muscles (of the Italian people) in joyful and simple sporting contests, to familiarise them once more with the glorious and charming traditions of their people, whether expressed in colourful costume, the harmony of song or a religious procession...To teach them and enthuse them with the love of music, song, dance, painting, sculpture, poetry, all the arts in which Italy has always led the way...

(Quoted in *Fascism* edited by Roger Griffin, Oxford University Press, 1995.)

It was also to be used for propaganda purposes and certificates were to be awarded to those who had shown 'noteworthy proficiency and activity in promoting the aims and objects of the organisation'. *Dopolavoro* certainly covered a wide spectrum of activities that included the provision of libraries, providing radio sets, showing films, sponsoring theatre groups and bands, and providing sports stadia and gymnasia. It also organized trips, excursions and holidays, provided clubhouses for local communities and distributed food and clothing to the poor. Free holidays were provided for members of the Fascist youth movement that often involved lengthy stays in the countryside in centres run by the *Donne Fasciste* organization. During this time they received free and thorough medical examinations. It was financed partly by public subscription and partly by a subsidy paid by employers and the State. Not surprisingly, it became very popular and in 1927, control of *Dopolavoro* passed to the Fascist Party. By 1939, its membership exceeded 4 million and it provided 8,625 libraries and 1,350 theatres and sponsored 3,324 brass bands and 2,208 dramatic societies. A sad feature was that the facilities provided by *Dopolavoro* were more readily available to those living in urban areas than those in remote rural villages. Even so, villages were provided with community centres with bars and billiard tables and these sometimes challenged or even replaced the local Catholic church as the centre of community life. *Dopolavoro* might justifiably be considered one of the few real successes of Mussolini's Fascist regime probably because it concentrated more on leisure activities and relaxation rather than political indoctrination. However, there were those that regarded it as nothing more than a more subtle form of indoctrination and an attempt to compensate for the low wages and poor living conditions still endured by the peasantry.

Mussolini's switch to racist and anti-Semitic policies

At the start, Italy's Fascist regime did not appear to be racialist or anti-Semitic and Mussolini openly ridiculed Hitler's virulent persecution of the Jews and in 1932 boasted:

> Anti-Semitism does not exist in Italy. Italians of Jewish birth have shown themselves good citizens and they fought bravely in the war. Many of them occupy leading positions in the universities, the army and the banks.

Sadly his position was to change, although to start with his racism was merely another form of Italian nationalism, as was clear when he said:

> ...I love those of my race, those who speak my language, that share my customs, that share with me the same history...I have been involved in racism since 1922, but a racism of my own...the pride of belonging to this race born between the snows of the Alps and the fire of Etna... The elevation of Italian prestige, of the genius of our civilisation...

Even so, there had been elements of racialism in his colonial policies when he was prone to stress the superiority of Italy's culture over African tribalism and, as we shall see, he later claimed that there was a need to impose Italian culture on the native populations of Libya and Abyssinia. He was also known to boast that 'Italians were Aryans of a Mediterranean type'.

Italy's Jewish population totalled 57,000 and this represented less than 15 per cent of the total and some 10,000 were active members of the Fascist Party with two, Aldo Finzi and Guido Jung, holding prominent positions in the government. Italian Jews had long been absorbed into the country's way of life and had contributed to the country's prosperity and progress. *Il Duce*'s anti-Semitism first became apparent when in 1936 he showed a willingness to discriminate against Jews. However, it was following the start of Italy's alliance with Nazi Germany in 1937 that Hitler convinced him that the Jews were in league with the Bolsheviks and shared the aim of world domination that his campaign against Italian Jews intensified. It is possible that Mussolini wanted to prove that he could match or even exceed Hitler's anti-Semitic policies and he hoped that his actions would further cement the friendship between the two countries. In 1937, he caused great offence when he referred to the United States as 'a country of niggers and Jews' and claimed that by the end of the century 'the acid of Jewish corrosion' would destroy many European countries. Mussolini was also undoubtedly influenced by the fact that the Jewish brothers Carlo and Nello Rosselli, former Italian Socialists, were living in exile, criticizing the Fascist regime and openly recruiting Italians to fight in the civil war taking place in Spain.

The leading anti-Semite within the Italian Fascist party was Roberto Farinacci who staunchly supported his country's alliance with Germany and claimed that too many Jews had 'wormed their way into strategic positions in Italian life'. In 1938, the Fascists published the *Manifesto Degli Scienziati Razzisti*, the Manifesto of Racial Scientists which was supposedly the work of a group of scholars from Italy's most prestigious universities. In fact, Mussolini was the main contributor to the ten points set out that might well have been directly from the anti-racial ravings that appear in Hitler's *Mein Kampf*. The points included:

- The people of present-day Italy are of Aryan origin and their civilization is Aryan.
- ...the majority of our present 44 million Italians are descendants of the families that have been inhabiting Italy for a millennium.
- A pure 'Italian race' is already in existence...This ancient purity of blood is the Italian nation's greatest title of nobility.
- It is time for Italians to proclaim themselves racists... Italians should recognize that European characteristics are essentially different from all non-European races.
- The Jews do not belong to the Italian race...The Jews represent the only people that have never been assimilated in Italy, and this is because they are made up of non-European racial elements...
- The purely European physical and psychological characteristics of the Italians must not be altered in any way. Marriage is admissible only within the context of the European races...

The publication of the Manifesto was soon followed by an anti-Semitic press campaign when *La Vita Italiana* and *La Difesa Della Razza* published a series of articles that were blatantly racist whilst Giuseppe Bottai, a prominent Fascist intellectual, expressed the view that 'racism should be displayed to resist Jews'. From the Vatican, Pope Pius XI, who had earlier commended Mussolini for not copying Hitler's anti-Semitic policies, was the first to criticize Il *Duce*'s change of heart when he said 'it is not possible for a Christian to take part in anti-Semitism'.

Unfortunately, after 1939, his successor, Pope Pius XII, was far less outspoken and failed to make any criticism of the treatment of Jews in Germany, Italy and elsewhere. Another critic of Mussolini was one of his henchmen and leading Fascist, Italo Balbo, who was opposed to German influence in Italian affairs. This made no difference since his leader had always distrusted and suspected his loyalty. In 1940, Balbo died when the aircraft he was flying was shot accidentally by Italian anti-aircraft fire!

Prior to 1936, an estimated 3,000 German Jews had fled their homeland and taken refuge in Italy but Mussolini prevented this when he banned the further immigration of Jews from overseas. In 1938 came the *Il Diritto Razzista*, a Race Law that introduced measures intended to 'protect the Italian race'. In content, the Law was almost an exact copy of the Nuremberg Laws introduced by the Nazis in Germany two years earlier. The terms included the definition of a Jew as being a person born to parents who were both Jews, even if they did not practise the Jewish faith, and a person born to parents only one of which was a Jew. Amongst other measures taken against Italian Jews was a ban on their marriage to 'Italian citizens of the Aryan race' and people belonging to other races. In addition, Jews were not permitted to join the armed services, be a proprietor of a firm that employed more than 100 workers, have contracts with the defence industry or own land worth more than 5,000 lire. Finally, Jews could not act as guardians for minors or disabled people who were not Jews or employ Italians as servants.

Since Italians did not take kindly to their leader toadying to Hitler or the introduction of the new anti-Semitic measures, the Fascist authorities had difficulty getting people to apply the laws rigorously. You may recall that even Mussolini saw to it that his Jewish mistress, Margherita Sarfatti, managed to escape abroad and it was known that his sons took steps to hide their Jewish friends in their homes. In 1942 during the course of the Second World War, the evil Heinrich Himmler, the head of the German SS who supervised the Nazi concentration camps, went to Rome to urge Mussolini to deport Italian Jews to his extermination camps in Poland where they would be humanely treated. For once, *Il Duce* stood his ground and whilst he agreed to intern Italian Jews, he refused to deport them. Afterwards Himmler accused him of 'sentimental humanitarianism'. It was clear that the majority of Italians would not be willing executioners of the Jews and as the historian R. J. B. Bosworth has written:

To absolve Mussolini from any responsibility for the Holocaust as some Fascist nostalgics have done, is absurd. To understand him as a philosophically convinced anti-Semite or any form of racist is equally implausible. As Farinacci had the gumption to reveal, Fascist racism was more opportunist and short-term than fanatical. It was as hollow as were many other aspects of Mussolini's administration.

(From *Mussolini* by R. J. B. Bosworth, Hodder Headline, 2002.)

The extent to which Fascist race laws were applied can perhaps be gauged by comparing the survival rate of Italian Jews with other countries that experienced the Holocaust.

table 8 victims of the Nazi Holocaust			
	Jewish population (September 1939)	Number of Jews that survived	Percentage of Jews that survived
Poland	3,300,000	500,000	15%
Czechoslovakia	315,000	55,000	18%
Germany	210,000	40,000	19%
Yugoslavia	75,000	20,000	27%
Soviet Union	2,100,000	600,000	28%
Austria	60,000	20,000	33%
Italy	**57,000**	**42,000**	**74%**

Art and culture in Mussolini's Italy

Italians in the form of Romans, together with the Greeks, can fairly claim that their early civilizations were the nursery of European culture and during the years that followed, Italian painters, sculptors, composers and writers continued to predominate. What then of the Mussolini years? In 1972, Noberto Bobbio, an Italian political philosopher wrote 'Fascist culture never really existed in Italy.' Does that mean that during the years 1922 to 1944, Italy became a cultural backwater? In fairness, unlike Nazi Germany and Communist Russia, in Italy artists, writers and film makers did enjoy at least some minimal freedom of expression. In addition, whereas the oppressive regimes in Germany and Russia caused many artists and intellectuals to escape abroad, in Italy a goodly number chose to remain and whilst it is true that artistic and cultural activity may have declined under Fascism, it certainly did not disappear. As we have seen, the *Opera Nationale Dopolavoro* contributed significantly to popularizing Italian culture as did the *Ministreo Della Cultura Popolare*, or *Meninculpop*, which was responsible for cultural affairs after 1937. It is also worthy of note that Giacomo Puccini's *Turandot* was first performed in Milan in 1926 and that during this period the works of Pietro Mascagni, particularly the *Cavalleria Rusticana*, became popular worldwide. Although Beniamino Gigli, rated amongst the world's greatest tenors, died in 1921 others born during the Fascist period achieved equal fame. Alfredo Cocozza, better known as Mario Lanza, was born in Italy 1921 and later became a star of Hollywood musicals whilst even the present-day popular tenor, Luciano Pavarotti, born in 1931 spent his childhood living under Fascist rule. A leading novelist of the period was Grazia Deledda and she together with short-story writer Luigi Pirandello were awarded the Nobel Prize for Literature in 1927 and 1934. Amongst the most popular writers was Carlo Levi.

Born into a Jewish family, Carlo Levi qualified as a doctor and was also a noted artist and writer. He became an active member of the Socialist Party and in 1930, formed an anti-Fascist resistance movement, the *Giustizia e Liberta*. He survived until 1935 when he was arrested for his outspoken opposition to the Italian invasion of Abyssinia. For some years he lived in exile and worked as a doctor amongst the poor peasants in the village of Gaglaino. On his release, he moved to France and during the Second World War was forced to hide to avoid deportation. During this time, he wrote *Cristo Si E Feermato A Eboli* (Christ Stopped at Eboli), which was an account of his experiences at Gaglaino where he experienced the suffering of the Italian peasants at first hand. The book became an international best seller and later, after the war, Levi was elected to the Italian Senate. Another outstanding novelist, Ignazio Silone, fled Italy to win fame in Switzerland. Some authors and musicians intent on finding fame at all costs, rushed to join the Fascist Party and these included the composer, Giacomo Puccini who was amongst the first to congratulate Mussolini when he came to power in 1922.

Italian Futurism

In 1909, Filippo Marinetti, a poet and writer, founded the Italian Futurist movement. He made his ideas known in a manifesto, *Manifeste du Futurisme*, in 1909 and they were to influence literature as well as other branches of art. In his manifesto, he claimed that Futurism was a clarion call to those who had been 'wearing second hand clothes for too long'. His views represented an extreme reaction against what Marinetti regarded as the sentimentalism and romanticism of the bourgeoisie and he claimed that his views were 'a celebration of the machine age, glorifying war and favouring the growth of Fascism'. Unlike those who retained a fondness for the old and classical, Futurism favoured the advance of modern technology and exalted in such aspects of contemporary life as speed, noise, pollution and the growth of towns and cities. In his *Futurusmo e Fascismo* (Futurism and Fascism), Marinetti did not conceal his hatred of learning, academics and those things that were in the past when in 1914 he wrote:

> The war will sweep from power all her foes: diplomats, professors, philosophers, archaeologists, critics, cultural obsession, Greek, Latin, history, senilism, museums, libraries, the tourist industry. The war will promote gymnastics, sport, practical schools of agriculture, business and industry. The war will rejuvenate Italy, will enrich her with men of action, will force her to live no longer in the past, off the ruins and the mild climate, but off her own nationals' forces.

Marinelli's followers produced manifestos that covered architecture, music, painting, and sculpture as they tried to make Futurism relevant to all aspects of everyday life and it seemed as if they were trying to re-invent life and create 'a new race in the form of machine-extended man'. With regard to literature, Futurist writing was to contain no adjectives, adverbs or punctuation and phonetic spelling was considered acceptable. Futurist art, regarded as the forerunner of cubism and modernism, was intended to be 'forged out of the beauty of speed and the glorification of war'. As far as architecture was concerned, Futurism rejected ornamental styles in favour of what was plain and functional. Since it rejected the type of classical art and architecture associated with Ancient Rome, Futurism placed Fascists in something of a quandary and they chose to neither condemn it nor proclaim that it had to be adopted nationally. Surprisingly, in spite of his proclaimed hatred of academia, in 1929 Marinetti accepted membership of the Italian Royal Academy!

The cinema and radio

Mussolini would certainly have agreed with Stalin who described film making as 'the strongest art', by which he meant that the cinema was a great vehicle for conveying propaganda and this *Il Duce* exploited to the full. Although not of the highest quality, the Italian film industry produced a string of melodramas and comedies for general consumption and through the use of a board of censors, *L'Unione Cinematografica Educativa*, the Fascists ensured that there was a link between the plot of each film and their politics. In 1933, a law was passed that made it illegal to dub Italian films into a foreign language whilst all foreign films had to be dubbed into Italian whilst films thought unsuitable were modified rather than banned. In 1935, the *Ente Nazionale Industrie Cinemato Grafiche* became the most important body in the Italian film industry when it became responsible for regulating the use of foreign films in Italian cinemas. As cinema going increased in popularity, so cinema box office takings accounted for 50 per cent of the income from all entertainment and this rose to 70 per cent in 1936 and 83 per cent in 1941. Mussolini's son, Vittorio, was involved in the film industry and the 1930s and 1940s saw the emergence of many future illustrious Italian film directors and producers. These included Roberto Rossellini, who made propaganda films for the Italian navy, Vittorio de Sica (born 1901), Carlo Ponti (born 1910) who in 1965 became famous for the production of *Doctor Zhivago*, Frederico Fellini (born 1920) and Franco Zeffirelli (born 1923). Mario Camerini's film of 1935, *Daro Un Milione* is still considered one of the best 1,000 films of all times.

It is also interesting to note that during the time when thousands of Italians left their homeland in search of better opportunities abroad, many that emigrated to the United States made their reputations as restaurateurs and in the catering trade generally whilst others found fame as actors, singers and entertainers. Amongst the most celebrated was Randolpho Di Valtentina D'Antonguolla who, as Rudolph Valentino, became a screen idol of the silent film era. Others included the popular singers

Pierino Como (born 1912) whose family emigrated from Palena, Dino Crocetti (born 1917), the son of an immigrant barber who achieved fame as Dean Martin, Francis Sinatra (born 1915) whose father was Sicilian and mother a Genoan, and Antonio Beneditto (born 1926) who became known as Tony Bennett. The famous bandleader, Anunzio Mantovani (born 1905) was the son of the principal violist at La Scala, Milan.

In Italy, radio broadcasting began in 1924 and expanded rapidly during the Fascist period. The authorities followed the example set by the BBC and granted a monopoly in broadcasting to one company, the *Unione Radiofonica Italiana* or URI that in 1927 became the EIAR. Radios known as *Radiobalilla* were mass-produced but because of the needs of economic self-sufficiency, they were made cheaply and often proved unreliable. *Dopolavoro* helped to popularize broadcasting and made radios widely available to the general public and in isolated areas, loudspeakers were set up in piazzas, market places, schools, factories and public meeting places. By 1942, an estimated 2 million Italians regularly listened to the radio. Of course, many of the programmes were dictated by the needs of Fascist propaganda but much against Mussolini's wishes, many tuned into foreign radio stations in order to hear accurate broadcasts of the news for themselves. The Vatican radio was also a good source of information as was its newspaper, *Osservatore Romano*.

09 the Italian economy

This chapter will cover:
- the economic condition of Italy
- corporatism and the creation of the Corporate State
- the battle for the lira
- the struggle to achieve autarky
- the impact of the world recession of the 1930s
- the introduction of public works schemes.

'The mystifying aspect of corporatism lay in its pretense of being able to mask class conflict for the superior benefit of the nation.'
(A view of corporatism expressed by Marco Palla in *Mussolini and Fascism*, Interlink Books, 2000.)

Although he boasted of being an expert on most subjects, the truth was that neither Mussolini nor any of the Fascist hierarchy had any depth of knowledge of economics and national finance. As a result, when *Il Duce* made known his future plans for the Italian economy, they were, at best, promises based on broad generalizations that contained little substance. At the third Fascist conference held in 1921 before the Fascists came to power, he stated that his future plan was the 'preparation of an organic plan for public works to conform to the nation's new economic, technical and military needs'. Even more lacking in detail was his speech to the Senate in 1923 when he said that one of his aims was to make the people of Italy prosperous. A subtle reference to the connection between the economy and the need to impose a Fascist dictatorship on the people came when he said 'There is freedom in prosperity that is not the freedom to be allowed in times of poverty.'

When the Fascists came to power in 1922 they inherited many problems. Italy was still a technically backward country with its industrial development proceeding at a slower pace than elsewhere in Europe. In rural areas, low living standards and poverty still blighted the lives of the peasantry and there remained those difficulties associated with the First World War – employment, industrial unrest and shortages. All these problems were further aggravated by the fact that Italy also had a rapidly growing population and it was not long before the Fascist regime added difficulties of its own making.

table 9 the continued growth of Italy's population

Total population (millions)		Major towns and cities (thousands)		
			1900	1950
1911	35.4	Rome	463	1,652
1931	40.3	Genoa	235	648
1951	46.7	Milan	493	1,260
		Turin	336	771
		Naples	564	1,011
		Palermo	336	711

Mussolini's real ambition was to make Italy increasingly self-sufficient and develop its economy along the lines that would allow it, in the long run, to achieve its full military potential and so make it possible for it to engage in wars of colonial conquest.

The economic condition of Italy

In common with most other European countries, during the period 1922–5, Italy enjoyed an economic upturn. On coming to power, Mussolini appointed Alberto de Stafani, a university scholar and economist, as Finance Minister. Determined to restore some semblance of order and balance to the nation's budget, de Stefani followed traditional laissez-faire policies and kept state interference in industry and commerce to a minimum. He reduced taxation, cut public spending, removed regulations and trade restrictions and encouraged investment. He was against protectionism and paying subsidies since he wanted businesses to compete with each other on an equal footing. His policies appeared to be working but this did not please Mussolini since what was good for the Italian economy was not necessarily good for his intention of turning the country into a totalitarian Fascist state. By 1925, policy disagreements had arisen and in the end Stefani was sacked and replaced by the industrialist and banker, Count Giuseppe Volpi. From now on the country's economy would be run with one purpose in mind – to bring it within the framework of the Fascist State.

Corporatism and the Corporate State

The idea of corporatism as a means of eliminating class conflict was based on many different and often unrelated and contradictory strands of political and economic thinking. The idea of Catholic guilds in which men and their masters co-operated, had been detailed in Pope Leo XIII's encyclical of 1891 which dealt with the condition of the working classes. The syndicalist views of the French philosopher, Georges Sorel, went further and recommended the establishment of worker-controlled industries. Edmondo Rossoni who wanted to prepare Italians for 'the life of tomorrow that would create a new social order that would last for centuries to come' took up these ideas and the Fascist theorist, Giuseppe Bottai, destined to be the first Minister of Corporations, also supported the corporate idea. However, within the Fascist hierarchy there were differences of opinion since, whilst Michele Bianchi and Edmondo Rossoni regarded corporatism as a means of winning the popular support of the working classes, Roberto Farinacci considered it a means of bringing workers directly under the control of the Fascist Party.

Whatever the differences, Mussolini saw corporatism as a way of bringing about the political and economic integration of Italy under Fascist leadership. Each corporation was to represent members of a particular trade, industry or profession and it was Mussolini's hope that his plan would eliminate the need for strike action, bring about industrial peace and an end to class warfare. More important, he was optimistic that his plan would create a sound economy capable of supporting his colonial ambitions.

The structure of the Corporate State

In 1926, the Ministry of Corporations was established by royal decree and this survived until 1934 when a National Council for Corporations came into being. The Corporate State was to be based on a complex network of organizations run by employers and workers at local, provincial and national level. Control of the network was in the hands of the National Council of Corporations but the Minister of Corporations would make the key policy decisions. To make the system work, Mussolini would need to win the support of the capitalist industrialists and bring the trade unions into line under Fascist control. In 1923, the Palazzo Chigi Pact was agreed between the employers' Confederation of Industry, the *Confidustria,* and the Confederation of Fascist Corporations that represented the workers. The Pact, which was really a statement of intent, stated:

> ...both labourers and industrialists can avoid the damages and losses caused by work interruptions if harmony between the various elements of production assures the continuity and tranquility of industrial development...a permanent Commission, consisting of five members from each side, will be appointed to supervise the fulfillment of the above mentioned principles...

In 1925, this was followed by the shrewdly contrived Vidoni Palace Pact by which the *Confidustria* agreed to deal only with Rossoni's Fascist trade unions, a measure that deprived the Socialist and Catholic trade unions of their negotiating powers and in reality made them obsolete. In future, representatives of the employers and officials of the Fascist Labour Corporations would carry out industrial bargaining and this was clearly to the advantage of the employers since it denied the workers the right to be represented by their freely elected shop stewards who in the past had been so fierce and truculent in their defence of workers' interests. The following year, a new law was passed that prohibited strikes and lock-outs. A problem resulted from the fact that the International Labour Organisation, an agency of the League of Nations, was pledged to respecting the right of 'freedom of association'. Using his usual cunning, Mussolini got around this by allowing employers and employees who did not wish to join the Fascist Corporations to form their own unions and he then used the *squadristi* to hound them out of existence.

The 22 corporations created every aspect of the country's economy:

> grain production, vegetable, flower and fruit cultivation, wine and oil cultivation, livestock and fish, wood, textiles, clothing, metalworking, machinery, chemicals, liquid combustibles and fossil fuels, paper and publishing, building construction, water, gas and electricity, mining industries, glass and ceramics, internal communications, sea and air, entertainment, hostelries, professions and arts, and social care and credit.

Each comprised of representatives of employers and workers. Members paid their dues to their corporation and took their orders from their Fascist-appointed officials. The first controlling body, the Ministry of Corporations, had the power to draw up contracts, fix wages, consider disputes and enforce settlements. In a speech made in October 1926 to celebrate the fourth anniversary of the Fascist March on Rome, Mussolini was able to say:

> We have constituted a Corporate and Fascist State, the state of a national society, a State that concentrates and controls, harmonizes and tempers the interests of all social classes, which are thereby protected in equal measure. Whereas previously labour looked with diffidence upon the State labour was, in fact, outside the State, and considered the State an enemy...there is not one working Italian today who does not seek a place in his Corporation...

In 1927, the *Carta Del Lavoro*, the Labour Charter came into being that reaffirmed the supremacy of the State over the individual and made clear its support of the capitalist system. Its preference for private rather then the public ownership of the means of production became clear when Mussolini said 'The Corporate State considers private initiative in the field of production to be the most effective and most useful instrument in the national interest. The intervention of the State in economic production takes place only when private initiative is lacking, or is insufficient when the political interests of the State are involved.' The Charter also included provision for workers to enjoy the benefits of social insurance covering accident, sickness and unemployment, welfare benefits and additional pay for those involved in dangerous employment or working excessive hours.

In fact, Mussolini's prized system of corporations had many weaknesses and was to fall far short of its declared aims. To start with its organization created the need for a massive bureaucracy and many of its officials were inefficient, corrupt and, more often than not, both! It was often the case that money intended for economic development ended up in private hands. Again, the idea of equality between employers and workers was an illusion since the employers dominated the corporations and decisions they reached invariably favoured them. In other words, in spite of Mussolini's fine words, the capitalist system survived much as before.

What did the system of corporations actually achieve? The truth was that the system never really materialized let alone achieve the high aims of *Il Duce*. The conflict between the workers and their employers was suppressed rather than solved, workers lost their freedoms and, in spite of all the promises, their standard of living soon declined. In spite of the introduction of a series of programmes of public works, unemployment began to rise, working hours increased, wages fell and the country's gross national product fell. In 1936, Mussolini went as far as to admit that 'We are probably moving towards a period when humanity will exist on a lower standard of living.' Almost without exception, historians have been critical of Mussolini's Corporate State describing it variously as 'totally irrelevant', 'an elaborate piece of humbug', 'an elaborate façade behind which corruption and exploitation flourised', 'a sham aimed at suppressing the workers' and 'a system noted for its bureaucratic bungling'. As Marco Palla has written:

> The influence of the corporate state did not produce concrete results relating to the economic or military aspects of war related production, but it did serve to

mobilise many – in particular students and young intellectuals – who were searching for identity and recognition even as they were being psychologically prepared for a climate of permanent war.

(From *Mussolini and Fascism* by Marco Palla,
Interlink Books, 2000.)

Most critical was Palmiro Togliatti, the exiled leader of the Italian Communist Party. In a lecture given in Moscow he said:

Corporativism was organised only after all the democratic liberties had been liquidated, when the workers had been deprived of all representation, when all the political parties had been destroyed, when trade union freedom, freedom of the press, freedom of assembly had been liquidated... Corporativism is inconceivable without the existence of Fascism as a political dictatorship.

In spite of the fact that Mussolini had produced on paper a system that didn't work and was in fact little more than an elaborate fraud, clever propaganda hid the truth from the people and he appeared seemingly as popular as ever but he was not yet finished.

In 1939, the Fascist leader finally put an end to whatever traces remained of Italian democracy when he dissolved the Chamber of Deputies and set up in its place the Chamber of Fasci and Corporations.

The battle for the lira

As we have seen, the years 1922–5, the period when economic affairs were in the hands of Alberto de Stefani, represented a period of relative economic well-being when there was a recovery of trade and unemployment fell. This was not to last and by 1927 the ominous clouds of an approaching recession had appeared. As the lira came under increasing pressure so its value fell in value to 150 to the pound (£). Taking his now usual defiant line, instead of devaluing the lira, he told the Italian people 'I shall defend the Italian lira to my last breath – to my last drop of blood.' Then, more for reasons of national prestige than sound economics, he revalued the lira at 90 to the pound (£) and arranged for the lira to be measured against a fixed amount of gold by restoring the currency to the gold standard. This he hoped would prove that his Fascist regime was capable of reducing inflation and providing economic stability.

However, although those industries dependent on imported raw materials benefited from lower prices, the measures undertaken made Italian exports much more expensive in the world's markets, damaged her export trade and reduced the country's income from tourism.

table 10 Italian exports and imports 1922–38		
	Exports	**Imports**
1922	100	100
1925	194	100
1929	189	109
1932	142	72
1936	115	52
	(Base year 1922 = 100)	

The overall effect was to worsen the country's balance of payments situation – Italy's payments to other countries for goods and services received (imports) increased compared with payments received from other countries for goods and services sold to them (exports). This meant that Italian firms dependent on exports faced severe difficulties and Mussolini was forced to protect them from foreign competition by increasing the duties placed on imported goods (tariffs) so that Italians would be more inclined to buy home-produced goods. Of course, other countries simply retaliated and this made the situation even worse so that between 1925 and 1938, the total value of Italian exports fell by 49 per cent from 44,370 million lire to 21,750 million lire.

The struggle to achieve autarky

Bearing in mind that Germany's defeat in the First World War was due, in part, to the fact that a shortage of raw materials made it impossible for her economy to sustain her war effort, Mussolini was determined that Italy should achieve autarky, self-sufficiency, and be less dependent on foreign imports before he put into effect his plans for colonial expansion. Part of his campaign to achieve self-sufficiency was the Battle for Grain introduced in 1925.

To achieve self-sufficiency in grain, higher tariffs were imposed on imports, particularly wheat, which meant that Italians had to depend more on the home-produced product. Reduced imports, of course, also helped to reduce the deficit in the country's balance of payments. Both new and intensive and extensive methods of farming were used – intensive farming meant that the same land was repeatedly cultivated in order to increase the yield per hectare, extensive farming that land that had been previously unused was brought into cultivation. To assist hard pressed farmers, the Fascist regime made grants available for the purchase of machinery and fertilizers. To give his support, Mussolini sometimes appeared in person, stripped to the waist, driving a tractor or working alongside the farm labourers. The Battle for Grain was certainly successful since between 1925 and 1938, grain production virtually doubled from 4,479 million kilograms to 8,184 million kilograms.

table 11 the increase in the output of wheat (million kilograms)	
1912	5,690
1924	4,479
1938	8,184

Unfortunately, there was a downside since the concentration on grain production meant that the growing of other crops, particularly vines and olives, and animal husbandry were neglected. The 75 per cent fall in the import of wheat led to an increase in the price of flour and consequently the cost of bread and pasta.

Some regions in Italy were uncultivated marshland unsuitable for cultivation and, in some cases, malarial. The shortage of arable land made it necessary for the regime to introduce a programme of land reclamation. In addition to making more land available, the project, known as *Bonifica Intergrale*, would create work and in the long run make even more grain available. The most ambitious scheme undertaken was to drain the Pontine Marshes.

The Pontine Marshes covered an area of 780 square kilometres in central Italy between the Tyrrhenian Sea and the foothills of the Apennine mountains. Centuries earlier, the region had been fertile and populated but, left abandoned, it had lapsed into unhealthy marshes. The drainage scheme, that required an enormous effort by Italian engineers and labourers, was not finally completed until the 1930s. Afterwards, the land was divided into smallholdings and allocated to farmers for permanent settlement and rural towns such as Littoria (now Latina), Sabaudia, Pontinia, Aprilla and Pomezia were built in the area. The spectacular achievement provided Mussolini with yet another reason to boast of the achievements of Italian Fascism but other agricultural problems remained to be solved. Between 1926 and 1934, the plight of the peasantry had worsened with their real wages, the actual amount of goods and services that money will buy, fell by over 50 per cent. Consequently, thousands of desperate men left their villages to find work in the industrial towns and cities. Carlo Levi described the pitiful condition of those that lived in the rural areas:

> The peasants' homes were all alike, consisting of only one room that served as a kitchen, bedroom, and usually the quarters for the barnyard animals as well...On one side of the room was the stove; sticks brought in every day from the fields served as fuel, and the walls and ceilings were blackened with smoke. The only light was from the door. The room was almost entirely filled with an enormous bed...in it slept the family, father, mother, and children. The smallest of the children, before they were weaned, that is until they were three or four years old, were kept in little reed cradles or baskets hung from ceilings just above the bed....Under the bed slept the animals, and so the room was divided into layers: animals on the floor, people in the bed, and infants in the air. When I bent over a bed to listen to a patient's heart or give an injection to a woman whose teeth were chattering with fever or who was burning up with malaria, my head touched the hanging cradles, while frightened pigs and hens darted between my legs. But what never failed to strike me most of all...were the eyes of the two inseparable guardian angels that looked at me from the wall over the bed. On one side was the black, scowling face, with its large inhuman eyes of the Madonna of Viggiano; on the other a coloured print of (the American) President Roosevelt. I never saw other pictures or images other than these, not the King or the *Duce*...
>
> (From *Christ Stopped at Eboli* by Carlo Levi, Cassell & Co., 1948.)

Ironically, Carlo Levi was describing conditions at a time when the Fascist regime was trying to dissuade people from leaving the countryside for the towns by emphasizing 'the beauty of rural life'!

The impact on Italy of the world recession of the 1930s

As we have seen, by the introduction of corporatism and other economic policies, Mussolini had turned his back on his own socialist background and anti-capitalist views and instead looked for the support of the country's industrialists, businessmen and bankers. In common with most other European countries, Italy was badly affected by the worldwide depression that followed the Wall Street Crash in 1929 and extended into the 1930s but it has to be said that the country fared better than many other industrial powers. In Germany, unemployment soared to 7 million and the country witnessed the rise of Hitler and the Nazi Party. In the United States, unemployment reached 17 million and thousands were reduced to living in shanty towns or 'Hoovervilles'. In Britain, the total number of unemployed peaked at nearly 3 million and this led to hunger marches and the need for a National Government. By comparison, Italian unemployment rose to just over 1 million but many more were living in reduced circumstances caused by part-time employment.

It should be remembered that before the First World War, some Italian industries had flourished, won acclaim for their products and expanded into the world's markets. Such was the motor industry with the Fiat Company (*Fabbrica Italiana Di Automobili*) founded in 1899, Lancia (1906), Alfa Romeo (1907) and Maserati (1914) leading the way. In addition, the Pirelli Company, established by Giovanni Pirelli in 1872, had become famous for the manufactures of telegraph cables and tyres, Montecatini for chemicals and ILVA for steel products. As the impact of the depression began to be felt, steel production fell by 35 per cent, car production halved and the average national income fell from 3,079 lire to 1,868 lire, so Albino Volpi, the Finance Minister, introduced a series of deflationary and protectionist policies. He first reduced the wages of public employees by 12 per cent and increased both direct and indirect taxes so that, with less money to spend, prices began to fall and the country began to suffer a deflationary spiral. Industrialists reacted to this by forming cartels by merging together to gain the advantages of monopoly. Since they now controlled levels of output and influenced prices, they were able to drive their lesser rivals out of business or as one economist put it, 'the big fish ate the little fish'. In 1933, the *Institu Per La Ricosstruzione Industriale* (IRI), the Institute for Industrial Reconstruction, was set up to help businesses and banks that were in difficulty. The following year, the regime tried to make more work available by reducing the working week to 40 hours and this meant, that as rates of pay were not increased, many workers suffered pay cuts. The *Instituto Mobiliare Italiano* (IMI) was also set up to help industry by buying up worthless shares and granting long-term loans. In an effort to provide relief for workers who were victims of the recession, industrialists were made to pay a proportion of their profits to the Agencies for Welfare Activities which was distributed nationwide. Between them the IRI and IMI helped to ensure that Italian industry survived the recession as well as, if not better than, many other European countries.

Public works schemes

The use of public works schemes to reduce unemployment gave the Fascist regime the opportunity to realize some of its ambitious schemes for rejuvenating Italy. *Autostrada*s, the first motorway system in Europe, were built to connect major Italian towns and cities. Over 5,000 kilometres of the existing railway system was electrified and new lines and stations opened. By 1935, the increased use of hydroelectric power meant that the country was generating 12,600,000 kilowatts of electricity annually – much of that came from newly erected power stations in the Italian Alps. In order to provide the country with alternative sources of power and counter the country's chronic shortage of coal, new oil refineries were constructed. A great deal of investment was directed towards building and improving schools, hospitals, clinics, sports stadia, and high-rise flats for workers. In Rome, plans were made to restore the buildings that once represented the splendour of Ancient Rome – the Colosseum, the temples, columns, triumphal arches and the Appian Way.

10 Italian foreign policy 1922–40

This chapter will cover:
- the aims of Mussolini's foreign policy
- the Corfu crisis and its repercussions
- Mussolini – 'man of peace'?
- the impact on Fascist Italy of the rise of Nazi Germany
- the Italian invasion of Abyssinia
- international reaction
- Italy and the Spanish Civil War
- Hitler and Mussolini – the start of 'the brutal friendship'
- the Rome-Berlin Axis and the Pact of Steel.

'It is destined that the Mediterranean should become ours, that Rome should be the directing city of civilisation in the whole of Western Europe.'

(From a speech made by Mussolini in 1936.)

We have considered the reasons for Italy's entry into the First World War, its conduct during the war and the bitter resentment at the terms imposed by the Treaty of St Germain in 1919. The post-war settlement that denied Italy the gains promised by the Treaty of London (1915) was considered a travesty by both D'Annunzio and Mussolini and labelled a 'mutilated victory'. Once in power, Mussolini assumed personal responsibility for Italian foreign policy but allowed himself to be influenced by Salvatore Contarini, the former Foreign Secretary. A skilful and moderate professional diplomat, Contarini was thought to have been a restraining influence on the Fascist leader. Although from time to time others held the title of Foreign Minister, Mussolini was always in charge and exercised control over all foreign policy decisions.

table 12 Italian Foreign Ministers, 1922–41	
1922–29	Benito Mussolini
1929–32	Dino Grandi
1932–36	Benito Mussolini
1936–40	Galeazzo Ciano
1940–43	Benito Mussolini

To a certain extent, many of the aims of Mussolini's foreign policy were clear but his intended means of achieving those aims were always uncertain since they followed no defined pattern based on well-considered ideas but varied according to Italy's changing circumstances. What was certain was that to achieve his aims, it would be necessary for him to establish a sound economy, increase Italy's military strength and enter into favourable alliances with other European powers. Mussolini would also have to show his skill as an opportunist and be able to recognize and take advantage of chances when they occurred. When in 1923, the British Foreign Secretary, Lord Curzon, asked Mussolini, 'What is your foreign policy?', he famously replied, 'My foreign policy is nothing for nothing.' On another occasion, he claimed that his foreign policy was 'to advance Italy's strength to the point where the Roman Empire was seen to be reborn'. Just how realistic were these aims?

The aims of Mussolini's foreign policy

Inflamed nationalism and rapacious imperialism together with self interest inspired Mussolini's foreign policy and high amongst his aims was the need to achieve great power status for Italy. In spite of the ill-will generated by the Treaty of St Germain, Italy remained on reasonably good terms with her former wartime allies, Britain and France and it was Mussolini's ambition to raise the status of Italy to at least their level. He privately held the view that both those countries were decadent and that the future lay with more vigorous and virile nations such as Fascist Italy. Mussolini realized that his drive to promote his country's prestige abroad might be blighted by Italy's armies' dismal failures during the First World War. The belated victory at Vittorio Veneto in 1918 had been won with the support of British and French forces and only went some way towards avenging the humiliation at Caporetto in 1917. It was also true that her former allies tended to consider that Italy had been a liability during the war and Mussolini was determined to remove his country's lame duck image. He set about doing this through the glorification of war. 'War,' so he claimed, 'alone brings up to the highest tension of all human energies and imposes the stamp of nobility upon the peoples who have the courage to make it.' Amongst the Italian people at large, bitterness remained about the post-war treaty that they thought cheated their country of its just rewards and Mussolini was very much aware that his reputation both at home and abroad would be enhanced if he could get the terms of St Germain revised. To this end, he employed the legend of a 'mutilated victory' to great effect as he strove to stir up nationalistic feelings. *Il Duce* also wanted Italy to become a major imperial power but with little territory in Africa or elsewhere left to colonize, this would prove difficult. Mussolini made it clear that he considered the Mediterranean Sea to be Mare Nostrum, 'Our Sea' and he was determined to achieve Italian dominance there but this too would prove difficult because of existing French and British interests in the area. France controlled the island of Corsica and the North African coastline stretching across Tunisia, Algeria and Morocco whilst the British possession of Gibraltar and the Suez Canal gave her control of strategic points of entry to the Mediterranean as well as important military bases in Malta and Cyprus. In 1919, Mussolini was clearly aware of their significance when he wrote in *Il Popolo d'Italiana* that Italy 'could tomorrow accomplish the task of bringing about the collapse of the British Empire in Asia and Africa'. He would need to tread carefully since France and Britain were still amongst the world's greatest naval powers.

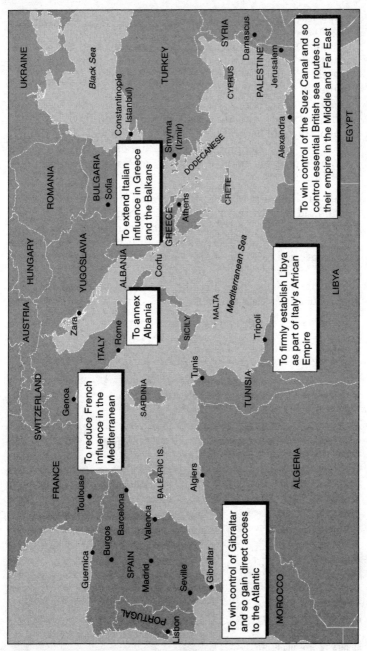

To extend Italian influence in Greece and the Balkans

To win control of the Suez Canal and so control essential British sea routes to their empire in the Middle and Far East

To annex Albania

To firmly establish Libya as part of Italy's African Empire

To reduce French influence in the Mediterranean

To win control of Gibraltar and so gain direct access to the Atlantic

figure 11 Italian ambitions in the Mediterranean

Disappointed by Italy's failure to gain control of Fiume and the Dalmatian Coast, Mussolini sought to extend Italian influence in the region of the Adriatic Sea and possibly even the Balkans. Particularly inviting was the prospect of winning control of Albania, a country that had formerly been part of the Turkish Empire. In 1921, Albania had become a republic under Ahmed Bey Zogu who, two years later, assumed the title King Zog. With the country already largely dependent on Italy, Mussolini thought it would be relatively easy to gain control of the country and use it as a stepping stone to extending influence in the Balkans where the main opposition to his plans would come from Greece.

In Africa, Italy already had the colonies of Libya, Eritrea and Somaliland but these in no way matched the great colonial empires of Britain and France on that continent. Any further territorial expansion there would be difficult since most of the continent had already been colonized by other European powers. However, there remained one opportunity, Abyssinia, where the Italians had already been decisively defeated and humiliated at Adowa in 1896.

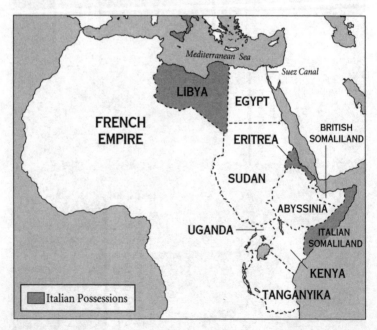

figure 12 existing Italian colonies in Africa

Some historians have argued that Mussolini's planned aggressive and adventurous foreign policy was not merely based on his need to enhance Italy's international status and acquire overseas territory, but was also his response to Italy's pressing economic problems. Such policies, he hoped, would distract the attention of the Italian people from the shortcomings and failures of Fascist domestic policies.

Remember that whatever foreign policy successes Mussolini might achieve would not only reflect on the quality of his leadership but also serve as glowing examples of the achievements of Fascism and this would help popularize that political creed abroad. There was, however, an unforeseen problem on the horizon, in 1933 another Fascist regime appeared in Europe, Nazi Germany. To what extent would Hitler's foreign policy ambitions affect Italy?

Mussolini's foreign policy ambitions were to have repercussions on the regime's domestic policy since to increase the size of the Italian armed forces and provide them with modern weapons would prove expensive and be a further drain on the country's limited resources. Whilst Italy's drive to achieve autarky had proved successful in limiting the import of grain, it had not gained similar successes with other raw materials so that the country remained short in essential war materials – oil, steel and explosives. With the Battle for Births in its early stages and destined to fail, Italy's manpower resources were to remain limited. In other words, Mussolini's Italy simply did not have the economic or military means to challenge for a place amongst the major powers and give Mussolini a voice in world affairs.

Italy's relations with other European powers

In spite of Mussolini's bellicose rantings, Fascist Italy faced no immediate threat from other powers. Inclined to unorthodox methods, *Il Duce* tried to exploit differences between France and Britain but Italy remained on reasonably good terms with both countries. As the two powers came to realize what he was up to, so he earned the distrust of both. Still, if Mussolini was intent on following an adventurous foreign policy, Italy would need the support of reliable friends. This caused the Fascist leader to begin a stampede to sign alliances and treaties with other European countries and these came in quick succession – with Poland, Czechoslovakia and Austria in 1922, the Soviet

Union and Switzerland in 1924 and Hungary, Spain, Albania and Greece in 1925. The treaties were largely commercial and of little importance, still Mussolini was always prepared to switch alliances when it was to Italy's advantage and, as the British ambassador in Rome, Sir Ronald Graham, commented, *Il Duce* was always prepared 'to offer Italian friendship to the highest bidder'. Still, in spite of all his posturing, the Italian leader remained a fringe player in European politics.

At home, with Soviet Russia in turmoil and the Italian Communist Party outlawed, the chances of a revolution had all but disappeared and Mussolini found ready support for his aggressive line in foreign policy. This came from stalwart Fascists, war veterans, those who had earlier enthused over D'Annunzio's exploits in Fiume, nationalists and members of the former *squadristi* keen to find opportunities to use terror and violence abroad. Of them, the historian Martin Blinkhorn has written, 'The resultant cocktail was a dangerously intoxicating one, especially when composed by someone so vain, capricious, violent and authoritarian as Mussolini.' Treading carefully, Mussolini first tried to achieve some of his aims through diplomacy. An example was his attempt to settle differences with the Greek and Yugoslav governments over Fiume and the Dodecanese that had been occupied by Italian troops since 1912 but the talks arranged came to nothing. Later in 1923, the Greeks feared that the Italian plan to reinforce their forces in the Dodecanese was a prelude to their formal annexation of the islands but Mussolini managed to convince other European powers that this was not the case. However, the image of Mussolini as a man of peace did not last for long and in 1923, a major crisis arose over the Greek island of Corfu.

The Corfu crisis of 1923

Albania had been independent of Turkey since 1912 and in 1921 the League of Nations had entrusted the guardianship of the country's independence to Italy. Albania had a common southern frontier with Greece and for some time there had been an on-going dispute about the exact location of that frontier. In 1921, the issue was placed before the League of Nations who referred it to a conference of the ambassadors of Britain, France, Italy and Japan who decided to send a commission to consider the issue. The commission, made up of Greeks, Albanians and Italians, was led by the Italian General, Enrico Tellini.

On 17 August 1923, a car containing Tellini and other Italian representatives was ambushed on a road close to Kakavia in Epirus on the Greek side of the frontier and the General and four others were killed. Although there was evidence to suggest that the assassins were Albanian, Mussolini overreacted by holding the Greek government responsible and sending an ultimatum to Athens that demanded an official apology for the crime and that members of the Greek government attend the funerals of the victims. In addition, he wanted the murderers apprehended within five days and executed, a salute by the Greek fleet to the Italian flag and the payment of an indemnity of 50 million lire. The Greek government was required to accept the terms within 24 hours and the indemnity within five days. The French Prime Minister, Raymond Poincaré, reacted to the excessive demands by describing them as 'extravagant – much worse than the ultimatum after Sarajevo'. In 1914, it was an assassination at Sarajevo that led indirectly to the outbreak of the First World War! The Greek government accepted most of the terms but refused to agree to the automatic execution of those responsible and thought the sum of 50 million excessive. They suggested that the League of Nations settle the amount.

Barely a fortnight later, an Italian fleet arrived off the coast of the Greek island of Corfu and Admiral Emilio Solari advised the authorities that the island would be occupied until the Greek authorities complied with all the demands of the ultimatum. He also demanded the lowering of the Greek flag. When this did not occur, the Italian battleships bombarded Corfu with some of the shells landing on an orphanage and refugee camp killing more than 16 people and leaving a further 30 wounded. The Italians then occupied the island.

International opinion was divided on the incident. Many foreign powers thought Mussolini's gunboat diplomacy impulsive and ill advised but there was also support for Italy, particularly in the British and French press. In London, *The Observer* applauded Mussolini's 'virile direction of his country's affairs' and in Rome, *Il Duce* told British reporters that her government would have reacted in exactly the same way if British soldiers had been murdered in Greece. Intolerant of the type of pacifist ideology of the League of Nations, he let it be known that he did not want the matter resolved by the League since he considered it outside its jurisdiction and that if it were, Italy would leave the organization. In the first international crisis he had faced, Mussolini was in a difficult position since, if he failed to get his way, it would reflect badly on his Fascist regime and public opinion might turn against him. As a British diplomat commented, 'the whole Fascist fabric might collapse like a pack of cards'. Then again, it might lead to international instability and encourage the re-emergence of Communist agitation. In the end, the League of Nations placed the matter in the hands of the Ambassadors' Conference that largely supported the Italian case and stated that the indemnity had to be paid. That settled, Italian forces withdrew from Corfu.

The Corfu crisis clearly ended in a victory for Mussolini and it seemed that his display of strength had allowed Italy's Fascist regime to win its first confrontation and this added to his popularity at home and prestige abroad. On the other hand, the crisis also showed that Fascist Italy's foreign policy was likely to represent a threat to peace and significantly the crisis also displayed the weakness of the League of Nations in dealing with acts of aggression. Neither were good omens for the future.

Mussolini – a man of peace?

After the squabble over Corfu had been settled, relations improved between Italy and Greece and there were signs that Mussolini was more inclined to honest statesmanship and had become a man of peace. However, Italy's continued friendship with Britain seemed less certain and in 1925 there was a hiccup in their relations when the Albanian government acted independently and granted the British owned Anglo-Persian Oil Company a concession to search for oil in the Adriatic Sea. The Italian government protested vigorously at what they regarded as an attempt by Britain to become involved in what they considered to be their sphere of influence. Again the issue was settled amicably when Italy was granted a 33 per cent interest in the concession. Mussolini was also concerned by the fact that France continued to offer political asylum to Italian anti-Fascists living in exile and he also disapproved of a French attempt to achieve collective security by setting up a system of alliances with Poland, Czechoslovakia and Yugoslavia. His reaction was to invite prominent European leaders to Rome in order to impress them with the achievements of Fascism. Then in 1924, Mussolini surprised many when he recognized the new Communist government in the Soviet Union. In 1925, in an effort to ease international tension, a conference of major European powers was called at Locarno in Switzerland.

The leading figures at Locarno were Aristide Briand and Austen Chamberlain, the foreign ministers of France and Britain, and Gustav Stresemann, the Chancellor of Germany. Mussolini, peeved because he wanted the conference to be held in Italy, declined to attend and sent Dino Grandi in his place. The conference was successful in that it confirmed Germany's western frontiers and reached agreement about that country's long-term eastern frontiers and Stresemann confirmed that whatever changes were required would be achieved through negotiation and not war. Mussolini, who was kept informed of developments by Grandi, was not over concerned about the impact of the meeting on Italian interests since he considered treaties as 'pieces of paper with no binding force if circumstances changed'. Suddenly he changed his mind and decided that he would make an appearance.

> Mussolini...arrived there in as dramatic a manner as possible – by speedboat and with his usual bodyguard of boisterous Fascists. The Italian press claimed that his arrival at the conference was the crucial factor in its success. No mention was made that he only attended one session for just a few minutes; nor that a hundred journalists boycotted his appearance in protest against Fascist brutality – only a few days earlier another of his murder squads had run amok in Florence, killing many innocent bystanders. He arrived at one press conference escorted by his usual crowd of Blackshirts, but the journalists refused to attend and waited outside the room to greet him in silent contempt as he emerged from the hotel lobby. This did not *stop Il Popolo d'Italiana* from describing how a large audience was deeply impressed by what he had to say. But never again did he invite a similar rebuff; henceforth, he preferred to stay at home.
>
> (From *Mussolini* by Denis Mack Smith, Weidenfeld, 1993.)

Although the agreements reached at Locarno did little more than reaffirm the frontiers agreed in Paris in 1919, the treaties did herald a period of peace based on international co-operation and brought with it a new optimism so that people spoke of 'the spirit of Locarno'. Mussolini's appearance, brief as it was, did create an opportunity for him to meet the British Foreign Secretary, Austen Chamberlain. As the two men discussed their countries' outstanding differences, they appeared to get on together and established a friendly relationship.

Another step towards promoting peace came in 1927 when Aristide Briand, the French Foreign Minister, suggested to Frank B. Kellogg, the American Secretary of State, that their two countries should set an example by openly rejecting war as a means of settling international disputes. Kellogg was not in favour of such an agreement between two nations and wanted to include as many others as possible. He was particularly keen to include Germany, who had only recently been admitted to membership of the League of Nations, and non-League powers such as the Soviet Union. To this end, a nine-power conference was held in Paris in 1928 where the signatories, including Count Gaetano Manzoni, the Italian ambassador to France, solemnly declared that their countries condemned 'recourse to war for the solution of international controversies' and renounced war 'as an instrument of national policy in their relations with one another'. Subsequently, a further 56 nations signed an agreement to abide by the principles outlined in the Kellogg-Briand Pact. As might be expected, Mussolini considered the agreement 'an absurd proposal' and he had no intention of abiding by its principles but this not prevent him from inviting the delegates to Rome to formally sign the Pact. As Italy continued with its preparations for war, Mussolini ridiculed the Pact as being 'so sublime that it could be called transcendental'.

The Kellogg-Briand Pact was idealistic rather than realistic and, since it merely repeated other earlier undertakings, it was not greeted with any great enthusiasm and was never to make any meaningful contribution to the future settlement of international disputes. The obvious weaknesses were that it had no means of enforcing its principles and gave no idea of the course of action to be taken against any nation that broke them.

Mussolini's reaction to the rise of Nazi Germany

Italy being a near neighbour, Mussolini was more concerned than most at the rise to power of Adolf Hitler and his National Socialists in Germany and he became increasingly alarmed when in 1933, the Nazi dictator withdrew Germany from the Disarmament Conference and the League of Nations. His unease at the turn of events led him to call a Four-Power Conference in Rome of representatives from Italy, France, Britain and Germany. From the start, discussions began to go badly wrong and little or no progress was made. Britain and

France were suspicious of Mussolini's motives and wondered if the calling of the Conference was a ploy to revise the terms of the Treaties of Versailles and St Germain whilst other lesser powers were concerned at their exclusion and the apparent disregard of their interests. The truth was that *Il Duce* was worried that he might have to increasingly share the limelight with Nazi Germany, a development of which he would certainly have disapproved. In spite of this, Fascist propagandists used the Conference to show that their leader was now playing a major role in European diplomacy. The Conference finally ended with the representatives initialling the proposals but there the matter ended and in the end, it all came to nothing.

Mussolini had mixed feelings about Adolf Hitler. He was flattered that the Italian press made favourable comparisons between them and that Hitler had stated that he was looking forward to meeting him. It was also known that the German Führer had a full size bust of *Il Duce* in his home and had said that the friendship between Germany and Italy 'would last for tens and tens of years or at least until I die'. However, once Hitler had consolidated his position as German dictator, difficulties arose between the two men. According to Nazi racial policy, Italians were Mediterranean-types and inferior to German Aryans and Anton Drexler, the original founder of the Nazi Party, did not help matters when he suggested that Mussolini was probably a Jew! Mussolini was far from happy at the prospect of the revival of German militarism and the prospect of having such a powerful neighbour.

The *Anschluss* – Hitler's proposed incorporation of Austria into Germany

The first real clash between Mussolini and Hitler came when *Il Duce* had to face the reality of Nazi Germany's territorial ambitions and in particular, the Nazi leader's ambition to bring about the *Anschluss*, the union of Germany and Austria. In order to guard against such a possibility, the Italian leader had already signed the Rome Protocol with Austria and Hungary by which each of the three countries agreed to provide military aid to each other should it ever be needed and as part of the deal, he had also undertaken to defend Austrian independence. Like Italy, France too was opposed to the *Anschluss* and their common fear of Germany drew the two countries closer together.

In Austria, there were those agitating for the incorporation of their country with Germany and in August 1933, Mussolini met

Engelbert Dollfuss, the Austrian Chancellor at Riccione in Italy to discuss the situation. Dollfuss, a long time admirer of *Il Duce*, undertook to take measures to establish a Fascist-type regime in his own country. On his return home and now safe under Mussolini's patronage, Dollfuss banned both the Communist and Austrian Nazi Parties claiming that his country was better off without 'Godless Reds and pagan Nazis' and set up the *Vaterlandische Front*, Fatherland Front, which was in effect an Austrian Fascist Party. To counter this, the Austrian Nazis intensified their campaign and turned to acts of sabotage and terror and with the situation rapidly getting out of hand, the Austrian army shelled working class districts in Vienna and engaged in street fighting. In June 1934, Hitler and Mussolini met for the first time at the Villa Pisani at Stra between Venice and Padua. The German leader turned up wearing civilian clothes and a shabby raincoat that Mussolini described as looking 'like a plumber in a mackintosh'. During their meeting, Hitler seemed content to spend most of the time quoting passages from his own, *Mein Kampf*, a book that *Il Duce* described as boring and one 'which I shall never be able to read'. Alone together, they spoke in German, the only language that Hitler could speak, and one of the languages that the Fascist leader spoke well. They discussed the issue of Austria and reached some agreement largely because Hitler agreed with most of Mussolini's demands.

The following month, the Austrian Nazis attempted to seize power by carrying out a putsch in Vienna where they forced their way into the Chancellery building and murdered Dollfuss. Fearing that the attempted putsch was a prelude to the German occupation of Austria, Mussolini ordered four divisions, some 40,000 troops to the frontier and made preparations to help if the country was invaded. At that time, Hitler was in no position to risk a confrontation and backed down. Mussolini, his reputation further enhanced and now widely regarded as the guardian of Austrian independence, soon had another crisis to deal with.

On 9 October 1934, King Alexander of Yugoslavia was assassinated in Marseille at the start of a state visit to France. The assassin, who used the name Petrus Kelemen as one of his many aliases, was a Macedonian and a professional hit-man employed by Ustasi, a Croat secret society opposed to the domination of their country by a predominantly Serbian government. Since many Ustasi had been living in exile in Hungary, the Yugoslav authorities blamed that country for the murder of their king. As other European countries took sides with Romania backing Yugoslavia and Italy supporting Hungary, so there seemed a distinct possibility of a European war. As negotiations were opened between the two sides, so the tension eased and in the end, Hungary did accept responsibility for harbouring members of the Ustasi and undertook to keep a closer watch over the activities of Croat refugees in future. Afterwards, much blame was attached to the French government for failing to provide adequate security for King Alexander's visit and it was also discovered that the Italian authorities had been financing the Ustasi and providing them with training facilities.

The ending of the Austrian crisis in 1934 did not ease Mussolini's concern about Nazi Germany's territorial ambitions and these increased when Hitler announced his intention to disregard the limits imposed on German armaments by the Treaty of Versailles, and to begin to rearm and introduce conscription. An anxious Mussolini reacted by calling for a meeting with the heads of state of Britain and France.

Mussolini and Ramsay MacDonald and Pierre-Etienne Flandin, the prime ministers of Britain and France attended the meeting, held in Italy at Stresa on the shores of Lake Maggiore. They protested vigorously against Hitler's decision to rearm and discussed the possibility of forming a common front to oppose any future German aggression and in *The Times*, Ramsay MacDonald hopefully claimed that 'now nothing could come between the three powers'. The so-called Stresa Front was short lived and the Conference achieved little apart from furthering Mussolini's reputation as a statesman of international standing. Yet, within months, the Fascist leader was himself preparing for an act of aggression that was to have catastrophic consequences.

The Italian invasion of Abyssinia

In diplomatic circles, the fact that Mussolini was preparing to invade Abyssinia was well known but the world was taken by surprise when, on 3 October 1935, Italian troops crossed from their bases in Eritrea and Italian Somaliland to begin the invasion of that country.

Abyssinia, together with Liberia on the west coast, were the only two remaining countries in Africa that had not been claimed by colonies of European powers. Although Abyssinia had attracted the attention of the Portuguese, French and

British, the country had managed to retain its independence whilst an earlier attempt by the Italians to colonize the country had ended in grief in 1896 at the Battle of Adowa. The emperors of Abyssinia, who claimed direct descent from King Solomon and the Queen of Sheba, took the titles King of Kings and Lion of Judah and in 1930 the crown had passed to Ras Tafari who ruled as the Emperor Haile Selassie. Today there are those, mainly West Indians, who consider the Emperor to have been divine and, identified by their style of dress and plaited dreadlocks are known as Rastafarians.

Although Italy and Abyssinia had signed a treaty of friendship in 1928, relations between the two countries remained strained and there were frequent border incidents along their common frontiers in Eritrea and Italian Somaliland. Mussolini boasted that his purpose in invading Abyssinia was to 'bring civilisation to a barbaric country…unworthy of taking its place amongst civilised people' and called upon the Pope to bless his mission. In so doing, he ignored the fact that many Abyssinians were already Christians though not of the Roman Catholic variety. In reality, *Il Duce* had many motives for invading Abyssinia. The main reason was to win imperial status for Italy and so prove to the world that his country was the equal of Britain and France but he also wanted to avenge the humiliation of Adowa, exploit the country's natural resources and win markets for his country's exports. As Italy was overpopulated, Abyssinia might provide territory suitable for settlement by Italian emigrants. In addition, a successful war would stir up the patriotism of the Italian people, add to Mussolini's own prestige and help guarantee the continued support of the people for the Fascist regime. It might also divert the attention of Italians from the country's economic problems and their leaders unkept promises. Another overriding factor was that the time was right. Membership of the Stresa Front meant that, even if they didn't support his actions, Britain and France would remain neutral and uncritical. As Mussolini said, 'if London would not close both eyes as France had done, it would at least keep one eye closed'. As for Germany, in the hope that Hitler would give him a free hand for his Abyssinian venture and unknown to his Anglo-French allies, the Fascist leader had secretly informed the German Führer that it was intention to leave the Stresa Front and seek closer ties with Hitler's Reich.

In Rome, excitement heightened as the people displayed their enthusiasm for a war that seemed inevitable:

They wave their hands and handkerchiefs and shout and sing. Now and again a voice rising above the others cries '*Saluto al Duce*' (Hail Mussolini), and thousands of voices answer '*A noi*' (To use). Then they all repeat the chorus: '*Du-ce, Du-ce, Du-ce*'. Now and again voices rise above the others: '*A chi l'Abyssinia?*' (To whom Abyssinia?) and the reply comes in a chorus, '*A noi*' (To us).

(From an article by *The Times* correspondent in Italy, September 1935.)

The crisis finally exploded into war when Italian troops crossed the Abyssinian border and as a result of a clash at Wal Wal, an oasis some 80 kilometres inside the Abyssinian border, 100 Abyssinians and 30 Italians were killed. Immediately Mussolini rejected a League of Nations offer to mediate, claiming that Abyssinia was 'a barbarous and uncivilized state whose conduct placed it outside the Covenant of the League'. At home, Mussolini's bellicose oratory stirred up his countrymen's patriotic fervour as soldiers were given a hero's send off and their families promised their safe return, 'a war without tears'. From his place of exile in the countryside, Carlo Levi witnessed the reaction of the peasants to news of the invasion of Abyssinia:

October 3rd was a miserable sort of day…Twenty or twenty-five peasants, roped in by the *Carabinieri* [the police], stood woodenly in the square to listen to the historical announcement as it came over the radio…Don Luigi, the local Fascist leader, spoke from the balcony of the town hall. He spoke of the grandeur of Rome…the wolf that suckled Romulus and Remus, Caesar's legions, Roman civilisation and the Roman Empire which was about to be revived…Huddled against the wall below, the peasants listened in silence, shielding their eyes with their hands from the sun and looking, in their black suits, as dark and gloomy as bats.

(From *Christ Stopped at Eboli* by Carlo Levi, Cassell and Co., 1948.)

The Abyssinian army that faced the invading Italians was a ragged, largely untrained force of tribesmen armed with spears or at best outdated rifles. Their situation was not helped by a lack of unity amongst their tribal leaders and the fact that in battle they preferred to fight according to a prearranged and set plan when using guerrilla, hit-and-run tactics to engage the Italian army would have been more to their advantage. The

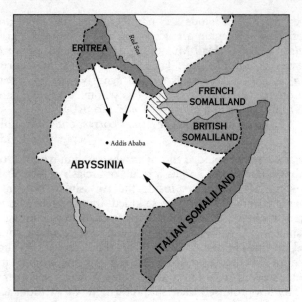

figure 13 the Italian invasion of Abyssinia

supreme commander of the Italian army was 69-year-old Emilio de Bono, a cautious but not very astute general. Before the war was over, he had to be replaced by the not much younger, 64-year-old Pietro Badoglio, one of the few Italian generals to emerge from the First World War with his reputation intact. Another commander who took part in the Abyssinian campaign was Rodolfo Graziani. They already had 60,000 soldiers at their disposal and in addition to these Mussolini intended sending a further 60,000 to 100,000 to ensure a swift and absolute victory. The soldiers they commanded were armed with modern small arms weapons backed by artillery, machine guns, tanks and aircraft. Later, the Italian decision to use chemical warfare in the form of flame-throwers and mustard gas, now outlawed by the Geneva Convention, against badly armed native soldiers and innocent civilians appalled many. During the course of the war, both sides were guilty of atrocities against prisoners of war and sadism was rife as men were subject to the most degrading forms of torture. From the start, it seemed that de Bono was more intent on capturing Adowa than winning the war and consequently a war that should have lasted a few weeks dragged on for over seven months. It was for this reason that Badoglio, who had specific orders from Mussolini to bring the war to a rapid and successful conclusion, replaced him.

THE AWFUL WARNING.

FRANCE AND ENGLAND
(together ?).
{ "WE DON'T WANT YOU TO FIGHT.
BUT, BY JINGO, IF YOU DO,
WE SHALL PROBABLY ISSUE A JOINT MEMORANDUM
SUGGESTING A MILD DISAPPROVAL OF YOU."

figure 14 a *Punch* cartoon of August 1935 ridicules the mild disapproval shown by Britain and France to Mussolini's aggression. Reproduced with permission of Punch Ltd.

Whilst the Italian invasion of Abyssinia appeared to meet with Nazi Germany's tacit approval, elsewhere it attracted worldwide criticism and the issue was placed before the League of Nations. Only a few months earlier, Sir Samuel Hoare, the British Foreign Secretary, had said:

> The League of Nations stands, and my country stands with it, for the collective maintenance of the Covenant in its entirety, and particularly for steady and collective resistance to all acts of unprovoked aggression...If risks for peace are to be run, they must be run by all.'

These were indeed empty words since neither Britain nor France took any positive action. Later, Winston Churchill wrote:

> Mussolini, like Hitler, regarded Britannia as a frightened, flabby old woman, who at worst would only bluster, and was incapable of making war. Lord Lloyd, who was on friendly terms with him [Mussolini], noted how he had been struck by the resolution of the Oxford undergraduates in 1933 refusing to 'fight for King and Country'.
>
> (From *The Second World War* by Winston Churchill, Cassell & Co, 1948.)

The League appeared to be taking decisive action when it stated that Italy had violated Article XII of the Covenant and declared the country an aggressor. It then imposed the only measure it had at its disposal by imposing economic sanctions that debarred members of the League from trading with Italy in materials likely to help her war effort. Quite amazingly, these did not include coal, steel and oil! Whilst Germany, no longer a member of the League, did not apply the sanctions, other nations continued to trade with Italy secretly. Britain and France might have considered closing the Suez Canal to Italian shipping but chose not to do so. In a way, the imposition of sanctions benefited Mussolini since it created a siege mentality amongst Italians that had a unifying effect and made them more willing to accept hardships. As a token of their resolve, women handed in their jewellery and wedding rings to help sustain the country's gold reserves.

In December 1935, Sir Samuel Hoare and Pierre Laval, the British and French Foreign Secretaries, put forward a compromise plan which they hoped would secure peace and maintain the alliance between members of the Stresa Front.

The Hoare-Laval Plan suggested a partition of Abyssinia that would allow Italy to make considerable territorial gains in the north, centre and south of the country and allow Haile Selassie to rule whatever was left – a small central band that included the capital Addis Ababa. For a time, it appeared that Mussolini was interested and thought it 'a possible basis for discussion' but this ended when the proposals were leaked to the press and the resultant public outcry forced the resignation of both Hoare and Laval.

In May 1936, with his country close to being overrun, Haile Selassie made a personal appearance before the League of Nations and, impressively dressed in his national costume, he spoke with emotion as he said:

> I, Haile Selassie, Emperor of Abyssinia, am here today to claim that justice which is due to my people and the assistance offered to it eight months ago. I assert that the problem is a much wider one than the removal of sanctions. It is not merely a settlement of Italian aggression. It is the very existence of the League of Nations. It is the value of promises made to small states that their independence be respected. God and history will remember your judgements.

Throughout his speech, the Italian delegates heckled him but his words did succeed in winning the verbal support of the United States and the Soviet Union. In the long run, the Emperor's words were to prove so very prophetic.

During May 1936, victorious Italian troops finally entered Addis Ababa and, although guerrilla war continued for a while, the war was virtually at an end. The Abyssinian Emperor, Haile Selassie, fled to Britain and left the Italians to impose their own government on what they now called Italian East Africa. In exile, he continued to campaign for justice for his country but this fell on deaf ears until 1940 when, during the Second World War, Italy sided with Germany. As we shall see, in May 1941, the Emperor returned to Addis Ababa in triumph.

For Mussolini, his success in Abyssinia boosted his image even further, seen as another triumph for Fascist Italy, his people readily accepted his claim that he had 'won the greatest colonial war in history' but there was a downside.

The impact of the Abyssinian war on Italy

As far as Italy was concerned, the cost of the war further drained the country's economic resources to the extent that the budget deficit rose from 2.5 million lire to a startling 16 million lire – an increase of 660 per cent. As pressure on the lire increased, so its value fell and by 1936 it had effectively been devalued by 40 per cent. These details did not appear in the Italian press! In addition, the Italian army in Abyssinia, over 3,000 kilometres away, was now involved in a guerrilla war that required the maintenance of an army of occupation of 250,000 men. This represented an additional financial burden. Contra to popular belief, Abyssinia was not rich in raw materials and the Italians only gained additional supplies of sugar cane, coffee and oil seeds and these were subject to the frequent invasion of crop destroying locusts. Mussolini's hopes of finding large quantities of oil proved a pipe dream. Even the Fascist regime's attempt to settle the country with Italian emigrants at the government's expense was a disaster since it proved excessively expensive and of the 130,000 that made the journey, many soon became disenchanted with life in East Africa and returned home.

Beyond Italy, her reputation had been damaged by a war that had cast her in the role of an aggressor and there was international outrage at the savagery used by the Italian army during the war. Even more significant to future hopes of peace was the League of Nation's failure to assert its authority and this was soon to give encouragement to others to attempt to achieve their aims by force of arms. Most damaging of all was the fact that the Abyssinian war brought with it a shift of power in Europe since Mussolini, offended by the failure of his traditional allies, Britain and France, to support his aggression, turned instead to Germany. As we shall see this was soon to prove a significant step towards the outbreak of another European war.

Italian involvement in the Spanish Civil War

In 1936, there was an army revolt against the Popular Front government of Manuel Azana in Spain. The revolt that was led by Generals Jose Sanjurjo and Francisco Franco and aimed to overthrow the legitimate left-wing government, was soon to turn into a full scale and bitterly fought civil war. Of the opposed sides, the Republicans represented the Socialists, Communists, Liberals, and trade unionists whilst the Nationalists drew their support from right-wing elements – the military, Church, capitalists, industrialists and the upper classes so that it was inevitable that the civil war soon turned into an ideological battleground. Both sides attracted support from overseas with the Republicans being backed by the Soviet Union and an army of foreign sympathizers, the International Brigade, and the Nationalists from Nazi Germany and Fascist Italy.

Whilst the German contribution to the Nationalists was considerable – 17,000 men and aircraft, Italy first sent only 12 aircraft to be used to ferry soldiers from the Canary Islands to the Spanish mainland. As the war progressed, Mussolini increased the Italian commitment considerably to over 75,000 men, who he claimed were volunteers, as well as 950 tanks and 700 aircraft.

table 13 the extent of foreign involvement in the Spanish Civil War				
	Men	Tanks	Artillery	Aircraft
Italy (aid to the Nationalists)	75,000	950	1,000	700
Germany (aid to the Nationalists)	16,000	200	1,000	600
Soviet Union (aid to the Republicans)	3,000	900	1,550	1,000

Il Duce's decision to become involved in the civil war was influenced by a number of considerations. He wanted to show that Italy was capable of standing shoulder to shoulder with Nazi Germany in the fight to prevent the advance of Communism in Europe and as he said 'Bolshevism in Spain means Bolshevism in France which means Bolshevism next door'. He was also anxious to support the establishment of another Fascist-type government in Europe and demonstrate once again the quality and fighting spirit of Italian soldiers. As with his Abyssinian venture, Mussolini again ended up on the winning side but at some considerable financial cost and an unexpected blow to his prestige. The war brought about a further devaluation of the lira and in battle, the performance of the Italian soldiers was far from impressive. At the Battle of Guadalajara, Italian regulars were routed and lost 2,000 dead and 4,000 wounded.

Embarrassingly, their humiliation was brought about by the Garibaldi Brigade, anti-Fascist Italians serving in the International Brigade!

During the course of the war, unidentified submarines operating in the Mediterranean began to sink ships destined for Republican held ports. The submarines involved were almost certainly Italian and some of the ships attacked were British and French. At a conference called at Nyon in Switzerland to discuss the issue, a brazen Mussolini was at his hypocritical best when he appeared to be upset and agreed that British and French warships should patrol the area. Afterwards the attacks ceased!

There were two other significant consequences of the war. Firstly, whereas up to that point Mussolini had always been considered the senior of the two Fascist dictators, it was now clear that Hitler was the undisputed master and in charge. Secondly, since foreign military aid provided by Germany and Italy had played a significant part in Franco's success, would he be prepared to repay them in any future conflict? As we shall see, surprisingly he was not!

Fascist Italy and Nazi Germany – 'the brutal friendship'

As we have seen, with Italian Fascism apparently triumphant and Mussolini moving towards an alliance with Nazi Germany, 1936 represented a watershed in the relations between the major European powers. The example set by Fascist Italy coupled with the failure of the League of Nations to respond encouraged others with similar aggressive intentions to follow and Hitler seized the opportunity to reoccupy the Rhineland. The Rhineland, a demilitarized strip of land to the west of the River Rhine, had acted as a buffer between France and Germany. The German action, which was in defiance of the terms of the Treaty of Versailles and against the 'spirit of Locarno', alarmed the French. Some British politicians, however, gave Hitler their tacit approval when they declared that the Germans were merely 'going into their own back garden'. Since France was not prepared to act without British support, Hitler's boldness had brought off a magnificent bluff.

Remember that in 1935, Germany had refused to apply the sanctions imposed on Italy by the League and had fought together on the side of the Nationalists during the Spanish Civil War. Now increasingly brought together by their common hatred of democracy and fear of encroaching Communism, Fascist Italy and Nazi Germany drew ever closer until they finally entered into an understanding, the Rome-Berlin Axis. It was in a speech made in Milan that Mussolini first used the term Rome-Berlin Axis when referring to the new understanding between the two countries. He said 'This Rome-Berlin line is…an axis around which we can revolve all those European states with a will to collaboration and peace.' It was part of the understanding that Italy would now concentrate on her foreign ambitions and allow Germany a free hand elsewhere in Europe. In Italy, there were many leading Fascists who disapproved of the German alliance but Mussolini hoped that Italy's close ties with Germany would impress, even frighten Britain and France so that they would treat him with greater respect. It was already known that Fascist agents were actively engaged in stirring up anti-British feeling in parts of the British Empire and in private and sometimes even in public, Mussolini made disparaging remarks about his former allies that he now considered as enemies. Such remarks as 'the British are people who think with their bums', the French are 'ruined by alcoholism and syphilis', the United States is 'a country of Jews and niggers' and the Soviet Union is 'a country that only cretins could admire' were typical of his contemptuous comments.

Italy joins the Anti-Comintern Pact

In 1937, Italy joined the anti-Comintern Pact. After the Bolshevik Revolution in Russia, Comintern (an acronym for Communist International), or the Third International, was founded by Lenin in Moscow in 1919 to encourage Communist revolutionary activities worldwide. By the use of propaganda and subversive activities, its members worked to undermine the political systems in capitalist countries and its long-term aim was to bring about a world revolution. In 1936, Nazi Germany and Japan agreed to work together to prevent the spread of Communism and formed an Anti-Comintern Pact. Mussolini's hatred of Communism made it inevitable that Fascist Italy would join the Pact and did so the following year.

During a visit to Germany, Mussolini made no secret of being impressed by German efficiency and military might and in a speech declared that Fascism and National Socialism represented 'the most authentic democracies existing in the present world'. The friendship between *Il Duce* and the Führer made it likely that Mussolini would be more tolerant of Hitler's intentions and accordingly the German leader revived his plans to bring about the *Anschluss*.

The crises over Austria and Czechoslovakia

In February 1938, Hitler summoned the Austrian Chancellor, Kurt von Schuschnigg, to his home at Berchtesgaden where he ranted and raved at his guest and presented him with demands which, if accepted, would bring to an end Austrian independence. Back in Vienna, Schuschnigg recovered his composure and bravely called upon the Austrian people to express their views in a plebiscite. Hitler was not prepared to risk the outcome of the plebiscite and on 12 March German troops marched into Austria. Hitler had advised Mussolini of his intentions the day before but this time, still unforgiving of the British and French reaction to his invasion of Abyssinia and unwilling to put his friendship with Hitler in jeopardy, he did nothing. Even so, many Italians were dismayed by his attitude and concerned at the prospect of having Nazi Germany as an immediate northern neighbour. They thought their leader had blundered and consequently Mussolini's prestige slumped. Some historians have come to regard this as the defining moment when Italy lost its independence and Mussolini's style of Fascism came to an end. Certainly the relative status of the two leaders had changed and now *Il Duce* was playing second fiddle and was subordinate to the more dominant Hitler who was no longer prepared to appear to be Mussolini's underling and disciple. However, privately the Fascist leader was far from happy with events and tried to retain a foot in both camps by signing a new treaty of friendship with Britain. Unfortunately new dark clouds soon appeared on the horizon as Hitler next turned his attention to Czechoslovakia.

As far as Czechoslovakia was concerned, Hitler's immediate aim was to annex a border region, the Sudetenland, which had a significant ethnic German population. As the crisis deepened, Neville Chamberlain, the British Prime Minister, asked Mussolini to use his influence with Hitler to arrange a conference to discuss the issue. Taken aback by Chamberlain's request, Mussolini concluded that Britain must be suffering from 'a menopausal disorder'. The Italian leader contacted the German Führer and after pledging him Italy's support, persuaded him to call off his threatened invasion of Czechoslovakia. During September, three conferences took place in turn at Berchtesgaden, Godesburg and Munich. As a result of the first meeting, Chamberlain and Edouard Daladier, the French Prime Minister, prevailed on the Czech government to cede to Germany those parts of the Sudetenland with more than 50 per cent German population. At the second meeting, Hitler raised his demands and with France and the Soviet Union likely to back Czechoslovakia, war seemed inevitable. As European powers began to mobilize their armed forces, a third conference was called at Munich attended by Hitler, Chamberlain, Daladier, Mussolini and his Foreign Minister and son-in-law, Count Ciano. The outcome was an infamous act of appeasement, a betrayal of Czechoslovakia and a surrender to virtually all Hitler's demands. The following month, German troops occupied the Sudetenland and five months later, in March 1939, Hitler broke all his undertakings and without informing Mussolini, invaded the remainder of Czechoslovakia.

Although Mussolini only played a minor role in these events, his Fascist propagandists claimed that his intervention had been decisive and portrayed him as a champion of peace and the saviour of Europe. The Czech crisis coincided with two other events – one relatively unimportant whilst the other had tragic consequences. In 1938, Mussolini instructed the Italian army to adopt the German goose-step style of marching which he claimed was impressively militaristic and during a public appearance, he actually demonstrated the goose-step which he said was unsuitable for 'the fat, the stupid and the so-called shorties'. During the same year, he decided to introduce Nazi racial policies and passed the Race Law.

During May 1938, Hitler made a second visit to Italy but this time in uniform and not in a shabby suit! During his visit, Mussolini set out to ensure that the Führer's reception was better than the one he had received earlier in Berlin. Impressive military displays were arranged though some German observers noticed that most of the guns seen were obsolete and some even made of wood! The visit certainly caused embarrassment:

> ...as constitutional head of state, King Victor Emmanuel was thrust into Hitler's company too often for the contentment of either. It was said that the King asked Hitler how many nails could be found in the German infantry boot and then illustrated his own pedantic knowledge of detail by explaining that in the Italian there were 74 (22 in the heel and 52 in the sole). Hitler later recalled that he had 'never seen anything worse' than the lugubrious (dismal) courtiers he met. The Vatican was also touchy about the visit...Pius XI made difficulties about providing illumination for one he condemned as 'the greatest enemy of Christ and the Church in modern times'.

> Meanwhile knowing Germans laughed at an Italian military exhibition in Naples where horses outnumbered tanks, whilst chief of police Bocchini took the occasion to sound out Nazis whom he thought might be in the know about the exact nature of Hitler's relationship with Eva Braun.

(From Mussolini by Richard Bosworth,
Hodder Headline, 2002.)

In November 1938, Mussolini called together the Grand Council to advise them of his future foreign policy plans that he described as 'the immediate goals of Fascist dynamism'. He also hinted that it was time to claim the Mediterranean Sea as an Italian Sea and remove the British controlled 'sentinels', Gibraltar and the Suez Canal. He said:

> Italy is bathed by a landlocked sea that communicates with the oceans through the Suez Canal, easily blocked, and the Straits of Gibraltar, dominated by the guns of Great Britain. Italy is therefore in truth a prisoner of the Mediterranean...The bars to the prison are Corsica, Tunis,

Malta, Cyprus. The sentinels of this prison are Gibraltar and Suez…Greece, Turkey, Egypt have been ready to form a chain with Great Britain and to complete the encirclement of Italy.

The annexation of Albania

He also had another concern. Hitler's successes in Austria and Czechoslovakia and Franco's impending victory in the Spanish Civil War meant that the other dictators were upstaging him. It was imperative for him to prove that he was not the inferior member of the Rome-Berlin Axis and to prove this with a spectacular success. Early in 1939, *Il Duce* sent an ultimatum to King Zog demanding the right of Italy to annex Albania. The King, who was offered money in exchange for his agreement, refused and rejected the ultimatum. In March, Italian troops crossed the Adriatic Sea to begin the invasion of Albania and although the Albanian army offered some resistance, the country was overrun in a day. In fact, 30 battalions of Italian regular soldiers were used and it was very much a case of using a sledgehammer to crack a nut! King Zog and his family fled first to Greece and then to Britain. As Victor Emmanuel assumed the Albanian crown, so a Fascist regime was established under Shefqet Verlaci. In fact, the invasion of Albania was an act of pointless bravado since the to all intents and purposes, the country was already under Italian control! Yet again, the cost of the invasion and the subsequent occupation of the country was to further drain Italy's resources and if Mussolini's purpose was to prove to Hitler that he too was capable of territorial expansion, then he badly miscalculated since by not first telling him of his intentions, the Führer was affronted. The occupation of Albania left Italy well placed to threaten Greece and Turkey but the British and French offer of military assistance to these countries if they were attacked, proved an impediment to further Italian aggression in the Balkans. Their action certainly annoyed Mussolini who regarded it as unwarranted interference in an Italian sphere of influence. Two months later, the existing understanding between Nazi Germany and Fascist Italy was replaced by a formal military alliance, a Pact of Steel.

The Pact of Steel of 1939

By the terms of the Pact of Steel, Germany and Italy agreed to 'keep in permanent contact with each other for the purpose of agreeing on all questions regarding their common interests'.

Further, if one became involved in a war, the other would come immediately to its aid and at the end of the conflict, neither would conclude an armistice without the full agreement of the other. Whether he realized it or not, Mussolini was in fact committing Italy to following a foreign policy that would be dictated by Hitler and the country was now committed to fighting beside Germany irrespective of the cause of the war – even if was the result of Nazi aggression! Although Hitler had stated that he had no intention of going to war for at least three years, yet a few hours after the Pact was signed, Hitler issued his generals with orders to prepare for the invasion of Poland. Behind the scenes, Count Ciano urged his father-in-law to make it clear to Hitler that Italy would not be in a position to fight a war until 1942 at the earliest and then Mussolini's anxiety was further increased when, in August 1939, Germany and the Soviet Union unexpectedly signed a non-aggression pact.

The Nazi-Soviet Pact, sometimes known after the signatories as the Ribbentrop-Molotov Pact, was an agreement between two countries practising the conflicting doctrines of National Socialism and Communism and was therefore clearly a temporary marriage of convenience. Since both countries pledged to remain neutral if the other became involved in a war, the path was now clear for Germany to embark on the invasion of Poland without the possible dilemma of having to fight a war on two fronts. Mussolini had no prior knowledge of the Pact and was puzzled since it seemed to contradict the Anti-Comintern Pact signed earlier. Whatever, Europe was on the brink of a war in which inevitably Italy must now be involved.

11

Italian involvement in the Second World War

This chapter will cover:
- the reasons for the entry of Italy into the war
- Italy's contribution to the war
- the home front and the impact of the war on the Italian people
- the growing opposition to Fascism in Italy
- disasters, collapse and Italy changes sides
- Pope Pius XII and the Holocaust.

'Who is going to win this war? You will say the best armed people. That is not enough. The people with the largest supplies of raw materials? Still not enough. The people with the greatest generals? Not even this. This war will be won by the armed forces with the deepest political understanding.'

(From a speech made by Mussolini in January 1943.)

On 1 September 1939, Germany invaded Poland and two days later, a British ultimatum was delivered demanding the withdrawal of German troops. When the ultimatum expired, Britain declared war on Germany and on the same afternoon, France joined Britain and the Second World War began. During this time, Hitler had not bothered to consult Mussolini, a sign of his increasing indifference to his partner. However, *Il Duce* did propose a conference to discuss the situation but Britain and France were in no mood for another Munich. This left the Italian leader in a quandary – should Italy fight at Germany's side as agreed in the Pact of Steel or find a face-saving excuse to stay neutral? He first declared that his country would adopt a policy of non-belligerency but did this mean that Italy would stay neutral or was he biding his time before making up his mind? In Italy, public opinion was divided about the war and some leading Fascists, including Balbo, De Bono and De Vecchi urged him to try and find a peaceful solution to the conflict. On the other hand, others like Farinacci pressed him to join the war without delay and described those who thought otherwise as 'honorary Jews', and 'cretinous opponents of the Axis'. Sections of the Italian press were openly critical of the Nazi-Soviet Pact but after the intervention of the German ambassador in Rome, such articles ceased to appear. Mussolini himself was far from happy with the direction of German foreign policy and uncertain that Germany could win the war, he continued to dither. Whilst Britain and France waged a propaganda war against Germany, no mention was made of Italy in the hope that this would encourage Mussolini to stay out of the war. The majority accepted that realistically, there seemed little doubt that once the time was right, he would side with Germany.

Italy's entry into the war

Following Hitler's move against Poland, Mussolini watched as the full weight of *blitzkrieg*, 'lightening war', allowed the Germans to advance across the country until, two weeks later and as agreed in the Nazi-Soviet Pact, Soviet forces invaded from the east and Polish resistance collapsed. The conquest of Poland completed, Hitler offered peace proposals to Britain and France but the Allies, as they were now called, refused unless the independence of Austria, Czechoslovakia and Poland were restored. For a time, attention from the war was diverted when in November 1939, the Soviet Union invaded Finland. In Italy and elsewhere there was considerable sympathy for the Finns and Mussolini sent military aid to help their war effort, as did Britain! Early in 1940, Mussolini and Hitler met at the Brenner Pass where the Fuhrer took the opportunity to explain his reasons for agreeing to the Nazi-Soviet Pact and *Il Duce* reaffirmed his intention of entering the war at the appropriate moment.

For some months there was little activity along the Western Front but the so-called 'phony war' came to an end in April 1940 when Hitler ordered the invasion of Denmark and Norway and the following month, Belgium, the Netherlands and Luxembourg before advancing across northern France. At this point, Winston Churchill, the new British Prime Minister, authorized the dispatch of a letter to Mussolini reminding him of their traditional friendship and urging him to stay out of the war. In his curt reply, the Fascist leader stated that Italy's friendship had ended when Britain took the lead in imposing sanctions on his country at the time of the Abyssinian conflict.

With the war continuing to go badly for Britain and France and when, at the end of May, the British Expeditionary Force was trapped at Dunkirk and France tottered on the edge of defeat, Paul Reynaud, the French Prime Minister, suggested to Churchill that Mussolini might be asked to mediate with Hitler. The British Prime Minister would have none of it.

With a German victory seeming imminent and Hitler in a position to dominate Europe, the war might be over before the Italian army played any part in it. In addition, with France defeated and Britain under attack Mussolini thought it a good opportunity to eliminate British and French influence in the Mediterranean and could wait no longer. The problem was that the Italian armed forces were still unprepared and ill equipped and it was questionable if the Italian economy had the capacity to fight another war.

In 1939, the Italian army consisted of 73 divisions comprising of 106 infantry regiments, 12 regiments of highly trained *bersaglieri,* ten of Alpine troops, 12 of cavalry, five of tanks,

figure 15 J. C. Walker's cartoon that appeared in the *South Wales Echo* on 5 October 1939 shows Hitler uncertain as to whether or not Mussolini will enter the war on Germany's side
© *South Wales Echo & Express*

32 of artillery and 19 of engineers. This was not as impressive as it might appear since only 19 of the 73 divisions were at full strength and of those, 14 were already serving abroad in Abyssinia, Tripoli and Albania. In addition, much of the infantry's weaponry was dated and not up to the demands of modern warfare and the tanks were light and inadequately armed. Although Mussolini boasted of an airforce of 3,000 planes, less than 1,000 actually existed. However, the Italian navy was quite formidable but limited by the lack of aircraft carriers now so essential in modern naval warfare and the fleet had only sufficient fuel to last a year.

During these last days when Italian entry into the war seemed increasingly certain, Mussolini received last minute pleas to remain neutral from King Victor Emmanuel III, Pope Pius XII and Franklin D. Roosevelt, the President of the United States and even some of his generals pleaded with him not to go to war. However, with France tottering before the German onslaught and unlikely to offer much resistance, the opportunity seemed too good to miss and on 10 June 1940, *Il Duce* declared war on Britain and France. Speaking to an enormous and excited crowd from the balcony of the Palazzo Venezia, Mussolini said:

Combatants of the land, sea and air! Blackshirts of the revolution and the legions! Men and women of Italy, of the Empire and the Kingdom of Albania! Listen! The hour of destiny is striking in the heavens of our fatherland. This is the hour of irrevocable decisions. The declaration of war has already been delivered to the ambassadors of Great Britain and France. Let us enter into the field opposed to the plutocratic and reactionary democracies of the West that, in every epoch have blocked our progress and frequently even stifled the Italian people...We take up arms to settle...the problem of our continental borders, that of our maritime frontiers: we want to break the restraints imposed by the territorial and military order that suffocates us in our seas... And we will win and finally gain a lasting peace with justice for Italy, Europe and the World.

In the square below, people cheered, youths sang uncouth songs against the British and French and chanted '*Du-ce, Du-ce, Du-ce*'. Of all his many blunders, Mussolini's decision to enter the war was to prove the most ill conceived. As we shall see, it was to lead to the collapse of Fascist Italy and his own brutal death.

Italy's contribution to the war

From the very start, the reality and full extent of Mussolini's blunder became apparent as his boast of having '8 million bayonets' at his disposal turned out to be closer to 3 million. Whilst thousands of young Fascists were indeed enthusiastic about the war and intent on great acts of heroism, many others felt betrayed by a regime that had duped them into fighting a war for which they had no heart.

After the declaration of war, Italian troops attempted the invasion of the French Riviera but only succeeded in occupying a few towns along the Franco-Italian border. Then, before an Italian offensive could really get going, France agreed an armistice with Nazi Germany and the towns of Modane and Briançon proved a scant reward for Mussolini's attempt to support Hitler by attacking his former ally and neighbour. It was in north and central Africa that Italian troops first faced the British when, against the advice of his generals, Mussolini ordered his troops to advance from Abyssinia into British Somaliland and elsewhere into the Sudan and Kenya. Even more adventurous was his plan to move forward from Libya into Egypt and so threaten Suez Canal. They managed to reach Sidi Barrani before the British counter-attacked, forced them to retreat 300 kilometres and took 100,000 Italian prisoners-of-war.

The Greek fiasco

A further major disaster of 1940 was Mussolini's decision, without Hitler's approval, to invade Greece. Offended by his paltry gains following the Italian invasion of France, he sent an ultimatum to the Greek government demanding the right to occupy strategic areas of their country for the duration of the war. When the Greek Prime Minister, Joannis Metaxas, rejected the ultimatum, Italian soldiers crossed from Albania to begin the invasion of his country. *Il Duce* was very much mistaken when he assumed that the Greeks would only offer token resistance and that Italian forces would occupy the country in two weeks. After some minimal success, the Italians failed to make further headway and when, in December, the Greeks counter-attacked, they forced their invaders back into Albania. It was said that Italian prisoners taken by the Greeks 'seemed untroubled by their plight and grinned at the bystanders as though thankful to be out of the fight'. Far from winning acclaim for Italian military might, the episode ended in humiliation that attracted the scorn of other nations and the disapproval of Hitler.

The failure of the Italian invasion of Greece was not Mussolini's only setback in 1940. In November, the British Fleet Air Arm attacked the Italian fleet based at Taranto. The base had inadequate anti-aircraft defences and during the hour long raid, torpedo carrying *Swordfish* aircraft sank the battleship *Littorio* and severely damaged the *Conte di Cavour* and *Caio Duilio* – half the battle strength of the Italian fleet. This crippling blow ensured the dominance of the Royal Navy in the Mediterranean.

The early months of 1941 brought yet more disasters for Italy in the Mediterranean as well as in Africa and Greece. In March, an Italian fleet under the command of Admiral Raffaello Riccardi was ordered to attack a British convoy bound for Greece with arms and supplies. Once again, the Italian fleet showed itself inadequately prepared to defend itself from air attack and once again torpedo-carrying aircraft caused havoc and inflicted heavy losses. In what was later described as 'one of the most sweeping British naval victories since the Battle of Trafalgar'; the Royal Navy proved itself the masters of the Mediterranean Sea.

In North Africa, although faced by an Italian army four times it size, the British drive across Libya continued as far as Benghazi at which point Mussolini had to ask for German assistance and accordingly Field Marshal Erwin Rommel and his Afrika Korps were dispatched to Libya. In what was to be the first of a series of to-and-fro campaigns, Rommel's offensive forced the British back into Egypt. Whilst to the south, the Italians were driven from both Italian Eritrea and Somaliland and in April, Haile Selassie was restored to the throne of Abyssinia. The situation in Greece was even more complex since if German troops were going to assist the Italians in Albania, they would need to send forces across neutral Yugoslavia. Prince Paul, Regent of Yugoslavia, was invited to meet Hitler at Berchtesgaden where he was pressed to join Germany and Italy, now generally referred to as the Axis powers, in the war and allow German troops to cross his country. On his return home, Prince Paul was overthrown by a coup led by officers sympathetic to Greece and the Allies and this caused Hitler to lose patience. As a result, he ordered the invasion of Yugoslavia and Greece and within two weeks both countries were overrun. As a result of the Italian failure, both Marshal Badoglio and Admiral Cavagnari were forced to resign their respective commands of the Italian army and navy.

Two other major events of 1941 that were, in the long run, to influence the outcome of the war were Hitler's decision to invade the Soviet Union in January of that year and, in December, the Japanese attack on the American Pacific Fleet at Pearl Harbor. Following the Japanese attack on Pearl Harbor, Germany and Italy both declared war on the United States. The war that *Il Duce* thought would be short lived and limited to Europe would now clearly be a lengthy, worldwide struggle.

At the start of 1942, the Axis powers decided to remove the constant thorn in their flesh in the Mediterranean, the British owned island of Malta. Situated to the south of Sicily and opposite Libya, British aircraft and ships based on the island were strategically placed to attack Axis shipping taking supplies and reinforcements to Libya. The island was equally well situated to act as a staging post for British convoys destined for Egypt. Throughout 1941, Italian and German aircraft had bombed the island incessantly and in 1942, Hitler decided to carry out Operation Hercules – the occupation of Malta. However, in order to concentrate on events in North Africa, the plan was set aside, at least for the time being. In North Africa,

Rommel's Afrika Korps had driven the British out of Libya and
back into Egypt so that by October, Axis forces were barely 160
kilometres from the Suez Canal. The German success and the
eclipse of the Italians upset Mussolini who accused his generals
of failing him and Graziani was ordered to appear before a court
of inquiry. Then in October, the British forces went on the
offensive and, following the Battle of El Alamein, the Axis armies
began a retreat and were driven right across Libya into Tunisia.
During November, Operation Torch saw American forces land in
Morocco and Algeria and this meant that German and Italian
forces were now trapped by Allied armies advancing from east
and west. In May 1943, the Axis forces in North Africa
surrendered and Mussolini's African empire was at an end.

During the early stages of Operation Barbarossa, the invasion of
Russia, in 1941 things went extremely well for the Axis forces
and Mussolini was proud that units of the Italian army had
contributed to this success. However, the severity of the Russian
winter took a heavy toll on the Axis forces who were unused to
and unprepared for such extreme conditions. The major turning
point in the war on the Eastern Front was the Battle of
Stalingrad fought between November 1942 and January 1943
during which the Russian Red Army first encircled and then
destroyed the Axis forces. The Russians took over 90,000
prisoners, some of them Italians, and few of them were to ever
see their homes again.

For Mussolini, 1943 was to be a grim year. Two months after
the surrender of the Axis forces in North Africa, the Allies began
Operation Husky, the invasion of Sicily. Although the Italian
army put up little resistance and civilians welcomed the Anglo-
American invaders, the Germans fought with great tenacity to
hold the island. Even so, after 39 days the island fell and the
Allied invasion of the Italian mainland now seemed imminent.

The impact of the war on the Italian people

The impact of war on the Italian people took two forms. Firstly,
in spite of the censorship of the media preventing the civilian
population from knowing the true extent of their country's
military defeats, rumour abounded. As the people became
increasingly aware of the failure of their army to win any
notable victories, they became disillusioned with the war and

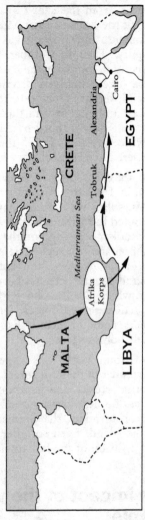

1940 Desert war began in September 1940 when 250,000 Italian troops commanded by Graziani invaded Egypt. Three months later, the British counter-attacked, drove the Italians out of Egypt and advanced into Libya as far as Benghazi.

March 1941 Reinforced by the arrival of Rommel and the German Afrika Korps, the Axis forces attacked and forced the British to retreat back into Egypt. The Germans however were unable to capture the port of Tobruk.

figure 16 the campaigns in the North African desert, 1940–3

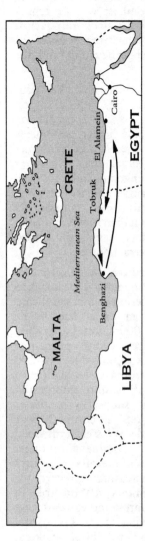

1941–2 In June, it was the British turn to attack and they were able to relieve Tobruk and regain most of the territory lost in March. Fortune next favoured Rommel and in January he more than repeated his success of the previous year when Axis forces advanced as far as El Alamein. He was now in a position to threaten the Suez Canal.

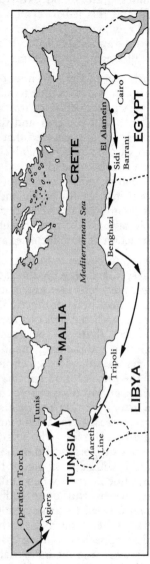

1942–3 In October 1942, the British launched an offensive, the Second Battle of El Alamein. The Germans and Italians were forced into a general retreat across Libya and into Tunisia. In November Allied forces landed in French North Africa and in May 1943 the Axis forces in North Africa surrendered.

this was reflected in a decline in their morale. In addition, Mussolini's oratory and extravagant bombast was no longer believed and this led to cynicism. Secondly, since Italy lacked essential raw materials and, in spite of the relative success of the Battle for Grain, had failed to become self-sufficient in food, the people suffered acute shortages.

Previously dependent on imports of German coal, her Axis partner's failure to continue to supply her needs had a knock-on effect on her production of iron and steel. By 1942, production had fallen by 20 per cent and this not only limited armaments production but also ensured that iron and steel based consumer products were no longer available to the general public. There was also an acute shortage of oil and of the limited quantity received from Romania, most was used for the country's military needs and there was little left for public and privately owned transport. As the war progressed, the Allied bombing of Italian towns and cities adversely affected the manufacture of war materials and caused the destruction of both factories and workers' housing.

In the countryside, shortages of artificial fertilizers and machinery together with the fact that so many peasants had been recruited into the armed services resulted in a significant fall in agricultural production. Food rationing had to be introduced with the aim of providing 1,000 calories a day per person, less than 20 per cent of the average peacetime consumption and the daily bread ration was limited to 150–200 grams per person. The government introduced legislation to control the price of food but this proved difficult to enforce and as luxury goods disappeared from the shops, so profiteers thrived in a rapidly expanding black market. The cost of the war led to an increase in taxation that affected all classes. It offended the middle classes who had been prominent amongst Mussolini's supporters and made the lives of the rural peasantry even more difficult. A sign of the increasing disregard for Fascism came in 1943 when 100,000 workers went on strike in northern towns and cities. Industrial unrest increased during 1944 and this led to strike action involving 350,000 industrial workers. When the Nazis threatened to shoot strikers, Mussolini appealed to their patriotism and begged them to return to work and the industrial unrest subsided. There is little doubt that the strikes were Communist inspired since they coincided with the recent return to Italy from the Soviet Union of Communist leader and agitator Palmiro Togliatti.

As the war progressed, the Fascist Party became increasingly remote from the people and appeared insensitive to their suffering. The people who had previously been all too aware of the Fascist corruption and inefficiency and had turned a blind eye, now became less tolerant and anti-Fascist literature and graffiti appeared in the streets. Mussolini, who had become something of a recluse and seldom appeared in public, became the butt of crude humour. Fascist bluff and propaganda no longer had any effect on the people and the truth of what was actually happening was becoming widely known as more and more people listened to Allied radio broadcasts.

Less recognized was the suffering of the many thousands of Italians who had earlier emigrated abroad. Many had lived in their adopted countries for decades, become thoroughly integrated within their communities and some had become well known and highly respected figures. Italy's entry into the war certainly changed that for many Italians living in Britain. Some, classified as enemy aliens, were interned. They had to appear before tribunals, had their freedom of travel curtailed and had to agree to do various forms of work before their liberty was restored. There were anti-Italian riots in London, Liverpool, Manchester, Edinburgh, Belfast and elsewhere and mobs threw stones at Italian owned property and ransacked and looted their shops. The irony was that the vast majority were anti-Fascist whilst some had taken British nationality and had husbands and sons serving in the British armed forces! A most tragic incident occurred on 2 July 1940 when a German U-boat operating in the waters off the coast of Ireland, torpedoed the *Arandora Star*, a Blue Star liner carrying German prisoners-of-war and Italian internees to Canada and as a result, 486 Italians were drowned. Following the United States entry into the war in 1941, tens of thousands of men of Italian origin volunteered to serve in the American armed forces.

Pope Pius XII and the Holocaust

A hangover from the war has been the controversy over the attitude of Pope Pius XII to the treatment of the Jews in Nazi Germany and Nazi occupied Europe. Eugenio Pacelli, who as a cardinal was the Vatican's representative in Weimar Germany, had witnessed the rise of Hitler's Nazi Party at first hand. In 1933, he had played an important role in the negotiations that led to a Concordat between the Roman Catholic Church and the Nazi regime by which Hitler promised Catholics freedom of belief and public worship. For its part, the Catholic Church agreed to stay out of politics. During 1939, the Pope made every effort to prevent war and even offered to mediate between the two sides and the following year did his best to keep Italy out of the war. The charge levelled against him was that he appeared to be indifferent to the suffering of the Jews and refused to speak out against Nazi atrocities and the genocide taking place across Europe. Most damaging to Pope Pius XII's reputation was the play, *The Deputy*, by the German Rolf Hochhuth that had its premiere in 1963 and the disclosures in the book *Hitler's Pope – The Secret History of Pius XII* by the British historian John Cornwell. In his book, Cornwell describes Pope Pius XII as 'arguably the most insidiously evil churchman in modern history who did more than fail to speak out against Nazi crimes – he supported Hitler's final solution'. Several Catholic historians have written in the pontiff's defence, so what is the truth?

It is certainly true that unlike his predecessor Pius XI, he never once criticized Hitler's racial policies. On the other hand, when still a cardinal he did speak out against Mussolini's racial laws in 1938 and the following year used his influence to get exit visas for 3,000 Jews to emigrate to Brazil but then they were all converts to Catholicism. Numerous world political figures pleaded with him to be more forthright in his condemnation but he argued that it was impossible to verify rumours about crimes being committed against the Jews. It should be remembered that the Pope's silence compared unfavourably with Catholic priests such as Alfred Delp and Clemens von Galen, who did have the courage to speak out. In addition, a great many Jews were given sanctuary by Catholic families and institutions with some 500 hidden in the Vatican and a further 4,200 taken in by monasteries and convents. In 1943, following the Allied invasion of Sicily, Pope Pius XII tried to get Rome declared an open city and so save it from Allied air attacks. In the same year, the Vatican part paid the ransom demanded by the head of the SS in Rome to save 8,000 Italian Jews from deportation.

Conflicting theories have been put forward to explain the Pope's behaviour ranging from Cornwell's conviction that Pius XII was an admirer of Hitler and was himself anti-Semitic to the view that he feared that if he spoke out, Hitler would turn on the Catholics. It has also been claimed he saw Nazi Germany as a bulwark against the advance of godless Bolshevism and simply sided with what he regarded as the lesser of two evils.

12

the final stages of the war and the end of Mussolini

This chapter will cover:
- Mussolini's dismissal by the Fascist Grand Council
- the Salo Republic
- the growth of opposition to what was left of the Fascist regime
- the final stages of the war in Italy
- the last days and fate of Mussolini
- an overview of Mussolini and the years of Fascist Italy.

'Judging events coldly, leaving aside all sentimentality, I have to admit that my friendship for Italy and for the *Duce*, could be added to my list of mistakes. It is visible that the Italian alliance rendered more service to the enemy than ourselves.'

(From *Hitler's Political Testament*, 1945.)

Mussolini overthrown

The defeat of their armies in North Africa followed by the speed with which the Allies captured Sicily increased the disillusionment of the Italian people and caused unease amongst the Fascist hierarchy and the commanders of the armed forces. On 16 July 1943, a group of senior Fascists still loyal to their leader including Carlo Scorza, the Party Secretary, Giacomo Acerbo, Giuseppe Bottai, Emilio de Bono, Cesare de Vecci and Roberto Farinacci asked for a meeting with Mussolini. They expressed their concern at the low morale of the people and asked that they be kept better informed about the course of the war whilst Bottai reminded *Il Duce* that the Grand Council had not met since December 1939!

Now faced with the prospect of ignominious defeat in the war, Dino Grandi drafted an agenda that proposed that the King assume the command of land, sea and air forces and the future conduct of the war should be placed in his hands. This was an open act of rebellion against Mussolini that would have been unthinkable earlier. In a long, rambling and often incoherent speech, the Fascist leader made excuses and reluctantly gave details of the Italian army's dismal failures before ending by reminding them that 'A war that goes badly is one man's war, but it is a people's war when it ends in victory.' At three the next morning a vote was taken and Grandi's proposals were approved by 19 votes to 8 with one abstention. Amongst those who voted for Mussolini's removal were Grandi, de Bono, de Vecchio, Marinelli and his son-in-law, Count Ciano. The vote of no confidence made it easier for King Victor Emmanuel and when he summoned Mussolini, the Fascist leader boldly claimed that the Grand Council was only an advisory body and had no power to remove him. The King replied that the Grand Council's vote was 'absolutely substantial'. Later, *Il Duce* claimed that his removal was the result of a plot involving the King, the bourgeoisie and the Freemasons. For a time, Mussolini, who appeared to accept his fate, was placed under arrest. The King's next move was to invite Pietro Badoglio to form a new government and in a radio broadcast to the nation, the marshal said:

> Let us close ranks around His Majesty, the King and Emperor, a living image of the fatherland and an example to all. The charge I have received is clear and precise, It will be scrupulously executed, and whoever deludes himself into thinking that he will be able to hamper the normal course of events, or attempt to upset public order will be punished.

However, Badoglio and the rebel members of the Grand Council would have been foolish to think that Mussolini was finished.

Badoglio's first act was to declare martial law across Italy and appoint a new cabinet that excluded any Fascists. At the same time he let it be known that there would be no mass arrests or trials of the former Fascist leaders. Since many thought that the removal of Mussolini would bring an immediate end to the war, there was much jubilation and rejoicing in the streets. Fascist insignia disappeared overnight as did black shirts and the *cimice*, a buttonhole badge that indicated membership of the Fascist Party and it would have been difficult to find people who would have admitted to being members of the Party. Shrewdly, Badoglio played for time by announcing his intention to continue in the war on Germany's side but, although carried out in secret, he had already started peace negotiations with the Allies. German intelligence became aware of this and this gave them the chance to strengthen their forces in Italy and so prolong the war by several months.

Early in September, Allied forces crossed the Straits of Messina at Reggio Calabria and landed in mainland Italy. Shortly afterwards, the Italian radio announced that Marshal Badoglio had asked the Allies for an armistice as King Victor Emmanuel and his government left Rome and abandoned central and northern Italy to the Germans. This led to the complete collapse of the Italian armies and whilst some remained loyal to their German allies, others either threw away their weapons and made their way home or opted to fight for the Allies. Uncertain of their loyalty, Italian units in German controlled areas were disbanded and some 600,000 sent to Germany as prisoners-of-war.

The Salo Republic

From a German point of view, Mussolini still had his uses since he could be used as a rallying point for Italians still loyal to their former Fascist dictator. Badoglio's government did its best to conceal where he was being held by regularly moving him from one place to another. It is said that Himmler used the services of an astrologer to try and locate him but in the end, the Germans intercepted a coded message indicating that Mussolini was being held at Campo Imperatore, a skiing centre high in the Gran Sasso. Hitler entrusted the task of freeing *Il Duce* to Captain Otto Skorzeny who with 100 airborne troops landed in a light aircraft close to the hotel and successfully completed a most audacious rescue attempt. *Il Duce* was first flown to Vienna and then on to Munich where he was reunited with his wife. Two days later he met the German Führer at Rastenburg and afterwards announced his intention of setting up a new Fascist government in northern Italy to be known as the *Repubblica Sociale Italiana*. Usually referred to as the Salo Republic since its headquarters was the small town of Salo on Lake Garda, the new republic quickly raised a National Republican Army, the *Esercito Nationale Repubblicano* of 150,000 men, and continued to fight on Germany's side against the Allies. Black Brigades, groups of still fanatical local Fascists, were created to enforce law and order within the Republic, round up deserters, persecute the Jews and fight against those who had joined the anti-Fascist resistance, the partisans. The Salo Republic had its own flag and produced its own postage stamps and currency. Although the surrender of the Italian navy was part of the terms Badoglio agreed with the Allies, some ships sailed to Spain where the crews asked to be interned whilst others, the *Marina Nazionale Repubblicana*, remained and joined Mussolini in the Salo Republic. Similarly, units of the Italian airforce, the most Fascist of the armed services, formed the *Aeronautica Nazionale Repubblicana* and continued to fight against the Allies. Now surrounded by the most fanatical Fascists and Nazi sympathizers, men such as Roberto Farinacci, Alessandro Pavolini and Renato Ricci, who urged Mussolini to declare Roman Catholicism the established religion of the Salo Republic and that all Jews were to be considered foreigners. Next Mussolini took his revenge on those members of the Grand Council that had voted against him and foolishly remained in the north of the country. His son-in-law, Galeazzo Ciano, was arrested by the Germans in Munich and flown to Verona to face trial. Later, together with de Bono, Marinelli and others, and in spite of appeals from his daughter, Edda, he was shot. A German report on the execution stated:

> The prisoners were made to sit back to front on a chair so that their backs were exposed to the firing squads...The only prisoner to cause trouble was Marinelli...The others maintained a calm demeanour. The firing squads took up their positions in two rows fifteen paces behind the prisoners, their small Italian rifles loaded and at the ready. At the word of command the men simultaneously opened fire on the prisoners, the front row from a kneeling, the back row from a standing position. Just before the order to fire was given one of the condemned men shouted: 'Long live Italy! Long live the *Duce*!' After the first salvo four of the prisoners fell to the ground, taking their chairs with them, while one remained sitting in his chair quite unaffected...The men lying on the ground had been so inaccurately hit that they were writhing and screaming. After a short embarrassed pause a few more shots were fired. Finally the cease-fire was given and the men were finished off with a pistol by the commander of the squad...

Before he faced the firing squad, Ciano wrote a letter intended for Winston Churchill that was not published until after the war. In it, he described his father-in-law as 'Hitler's tragic and vile puppet' and concluded 'the misfortune of Italy was not the fault of the people but due to the shameful behaviour of one man'. Edda never forgave her father and said, 'The Italian people must avenge the death of my husband. And if they do not, I will do it with my own hands.' In Salo, Mussolini, his wife, Rachele and their surviving children and grandchildren, lived in luxury and apparent domestic harmony in the Villa Feltrinelli but this was shattered by the arrival of the Fascist leader's young mistress, Clara Petacci. For all Mussolini's exaggerated claims, the Salo Republic only managed to encourage a part revival of Fascism in a limited region of northern Italy. Regrettably for the local Italian people, the struggle to defend the flank of the German line turned the area into a battleground.

During this time, Mussolini, who had always suffered from ulcers and gastric problems, began to suffer from poor health. For a time, a strict diet helped him to recover but then his troubles returned and he began to noticeably lose weight so that one observer described him as being 'reduced to a walking corpse'.

Italian resistance to Fascism, 1943–5

It was during the final years of the war that an effective anti-Fascist movement appeared in the German-occupied north. The slowness of the Allied advance caused groups of partisans to operate behind the German lines and attack units of Italian soldiers still loyal to Mussolini as well as harass German troop movements. The partisans, that were largely made up of ex-soldiers and escaped prisoners-of-war, soon attracted civilians from varied backgrounds. With 50,000 men at their disposal, the Communists formed the largest single group but Christian Democrats, Socialists and Liberals were also to be found amongst their ranks.

On his return from the Soviet Union, Palmiro Togliatti, the exiled Communist Party leader, agreed to collaborate with the King and Badoglio and with the help of the local peasantry, the partisans survived in the mountains from where they carried out acts of sabotage. As they grew in number, they became more daring and were prepared to engage German units in pitched battles. During this period, there were many atrocities and acts of retaliation committed by both sides and some used it as an opportunity to settle long-standing feuds and old family feuds. The Nazi authorities let it be known that for every German soldier killed, 50 local inhabitants would be executed and this resulted in the Ardeatine massacre.

In March 1944, Italian partisans killed 33 German soldiers. Within 24 hours Hitler ordered that ten Italians would be shot for every dead German and the execution of 335 civilians took place in the Ardeatine caves a short distance from Rome. After the war, the German responsible, Erich Priebke, managed to escape to Argentina where he remained for 50 years before being extradited back to Italy. At his trial, he pleaded: 'I gave Argentina fifty years of my life...I fought for Germany during the war, now they want to put me on trial for obeying orders.' Mussolini complained to the German commander, Albert Kesselring, about the atrocities but to no avail. Eventually a *Comitato Di Liberazione*, a Central Committee of National Liberation, was set up to co-ordinate resistance activities in northern Italy with the elderly former Prime Minister, Ivanoe Bonomi as its president. As the end of the war approached, the partisan army had grown to 250,000 and was strong enough to liberate such cities as Milan, Turin and Genoa ahead of the arrival of the Allies.

The end of the war

The Allied advance along the 1,200 kilometres of the Apennine mountains, the so-called 'backbone of Italy' was slow and hard fought and by the end of 1943, Kesselring had established a defensive line across Italy, the Gustav Line, that stretched from the estuary of the River Garigliano to the town of Pescara on the Adriatic. The line included the impressively built and heavily defended Benedictine monastery, Monte Cassino, which took weeks to capture. Finally the Allies outflanked the Gustav Line by landing further to the north at Anzio but it still took four months to break out and continue their advance towards Rome. Forced to retreat again, the Germans formed a new defensive line, the Gothic Line, which stretched across Italy from Spezia in the west to Rimini in the east. It was not until April 1945, that the Allies breached the Gothic Line to begin a final thrust towards the Alps. By this time the German retreat had turned into a rout and the war in Italy was as good as over.

The last days of Benito Mussolini

In these last days of his life, Benito Mussolini, pale, exhausted and a shadow of his former bombastic self, looked much older than his 62 years. Hitler had promised him that secret weapons were being developed that would still change the course of the war but *Il Duce* recognized that the promise was no more than an illusion. Unaware that the Central Committee of National Liberation had ordered that leading Fascists were to be executed without trial, he left his villa at Salo and headed for Milan. He said: 'I am close to the end...I await an epilogue for this tragedy in which I no longer have a part to play. I made a mistake and I shall pay for it.' He did consider negotiating with the resistance but was told that if he surrendered, he could only expect the 'ordinary guarantees given to prisoners of war'. When he was made aware that the Germans were fleeing from Italy, he raged: 'They have treated us like dogs, and in the end they have betrayed us.' On 25 April, Mussolini, Claretta Petacci and other leading Fascists spent the night in a farmhouse where he wrote a final letter to his wife:

> Here I am on the last lap of my life, at the last page of my book...I ask for your forgiveness for all the harm I have done you without wishing to. But you know that you are the only woman I have really loved.

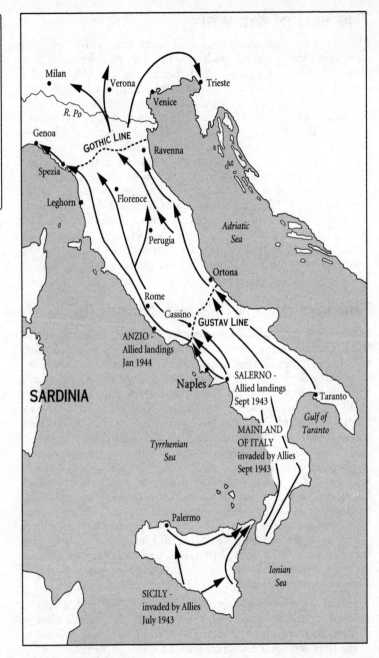

figure 17 the liberation of Italy

He advised his wife and children to either seek refuge in Switzerland or give themselves up to the Allies. He neglected to mention that his mistress was staying with him! The next morning the convoy of vehicles continued towards Menaggio and then joined other German vehicles heading north. At the village of Dongo, partisans halted the convoy who insisted on searching the vehicle and although dressed in German army uniform and pretending to be asleep, he was recognized. At first his captors seemed uncertain what to do with him but eventually he was taken to Azzano and there spent the last night of his life in the company of Claretta Petacci. The next morning, they were bundled into a car and after a short drive reached the front gates of the Villa Belmonte and there three gunmen shot them. Claretta Petacci, who refused to be separated from Mussolini, was also executed. Elsewhere, groups of leading Fascists were taken off and shot in groups, 15 at a time. The next day, the bodies of *Il Duce* and his mistress were taken into the centre of Milan were they were further mutilated by bystanders before being strung up by their feet from the girders of a garage roof in the Piazzale Loreto.

Two days later, Adolf Hitler and Eva Braun, his one-time mistress, now his wife, committed suicide in a Berlin bunker. On 8 May, the German armies surrendered and the Second World War in Europe was finally over.

As for the fate of Mussolini's family – his wife, Rachele, as well as his son, Romano, and daughter, Anna-Maria, were arrested by the Allies and were well cared for and later released. Rachele, who returned to her home town to run her family's estate, campaigned for many years for the release of her husband's body that had unceremoniously been moved from place to place but never given a permanent home. Her wish was finally granted in 1957 when his remains were buried in the family vault at Predappio. Rachele died in 1979. *Il Duce*'s elder surviving son, Vittorio, who had been an active Fascist, made his way to Argentina after the war where he was well received by Juan Peron, an admirer of Italian Fascism. In 1968, he returned to Italy and made documentary films about his father. For a time, Romano, who had never been involved in politics, found his musical career blighted by his infamous family name, but during the 1950s, he had regained his reputation and appeared regularly at jazz festivals. He had married Maria Scicolone, the sister of the actress Sophia Loren but the marriage ended in divorce. In more recent times their attractive daughter, Alessandrra Mussolini, achieved some notoriety by appearing in erotic films before being elected to the Italian Chamber of Deputies as a representative of the right-wing *Alleanza Nationale,* National Alliance Party. She boldly declared, 'I'm called Mussolini. I have a clear identity...and people love me or hate me.' After the execution of her husband, Edda, Mussolini's elder daughter, also made her way to Switzerland but rejected any attempt at reconciliation with her father. Ten years passed before she finally agreed to meet her mother and visit her father's tomb at Predappio. She lived a quite futile existence and died in 1995 of an alcohol related condition. Polio-stricken, Anna-Maria, married but had no children and died in 1968.

Mussolini's Fascist Italy – an overview

Because of his appearance and behaviour, Mussolini is an easy person to ridicule and lampoon. Whilst Winston Churchill once famously referred to him as 'the bullfrog of the Pontine Marches' and the historian A. J. P. Taylor as a 'vain blustering boaster', many historians have regarded him simply as a buffoon who even failed to get the Italian trains to run on time. Let us consider the views of historians:

> Everything about Fascism was a fraud; the social peril from which he saved Italy was a fraud; the revolution by which it seized power was a fraud; the ability and policy of Mussolini was fraudulent. Fascist rule was corrupt, incompetent, empty...
>
> (From *The Origins of the Second World War* by A. J. P. Taylor, Hamish Hamilton, 1965.)

His influence has been durable and not only inside Italy. Most people, but not all, would call his legacy disastrous. Though his Fascist regime may be credited with some positive achievements especially in its early years, its crude belief in political violence and authoritarian repression had negative effects that lasted long after 1945, and its praise of war as something inherently beautiful and beneficial was a cruel absurdity that did untold harm and ultimately turned any positive achievements to dust and ashes.

(From *Mussolini* by Denis Mack Smith, Weidenfeld & Nicholson, 1977.)

Ironically, Mussolini had succeeded in uniting Italians briefly – but against Fascism rather than for it. None the less the legacy of Fascism was to be far reaching, Quite apart from a disastrous war fought on Italian territory,

Fascism bequeathed poverty and inefficiency...and a political practice which had generalised petty corruption and made the use of public office for private gain the norm...The attempt to form a nation, to give Italians a single identity in the Italian State had proved a total failure.

(From Italy 1915–1945: Politics and Society by
Paul Corner, Oxford University Press, 1997.)

In total, then, it may be agreed that Mussolini was, in some sense, 'a man for all that', a personage who reflected his gender, class and nation, a tyrant of course, but not so vicious that history should relegate him to...some Dantesque hell... In the final analysis, the problem with Benito Amilcare Mussolini was that, for all his aspirations to exercise power, he turned out to be no more than an ambitious intellectual from the provinces who believed that his will mattered and who thought, as did others, that he was a *Duce* and could lead a state like Italy towards a special sort of modernisation. His protagonists thought that he was always right. However, in the most profound matters...he was, with little exception, wrong.

(From Mussolini by Richard Boswell,
Hodder Headline, 2002.)

Let us remember too that the conclusion of the war did not bring an end to Italian Fascism since neo-Fascist movements and the veneration of Mussolini still exists in Italy today. Maybe the following article that appeared in a British newspaper should serve as a warning:

A mayor in northern Italy is struggling to stop his town from becoming a mecca for Fascists from all over Europe amid signs that Italian right-wingers are rehabilitating the legacy of Benito Mussolini. Predappio, near Bologna, the birthplace and final resting place of *Il Duce* has long been a place of pilgrimage for Mussolini apologists. More than 100,000 people have visited in the past year...On Predappio's main street, souvenir shops enjoy a burgeoning trade in Mussolini paraphernalia despite a law banning the public glorification of Fascism. In addition to *Il Duce* flags, badges, posters and calendars, the shops sell CDs of Fascist songs...A woman buying a Mussolini calendar said that his only fault was that he lost the war.

(From an article in the British newspaper,
The Independent, by Kate Goldberg, July 2002.)

glossary

anarchist A person whose ideal society is one without government and advances his aims with terrorism.

Aryans North European type of Caucasian.

autarky Self-sufficiency.

authoritarian Setting authority above liberty.

autocratic Absolute government by one person.

Axis powers Wartime alliance between Nazi Germany and Fascist Italy.

balance of payments Difference between nations total receipts from foreign countries and payments to foreign countries.

Bersaglieri Regiment of highly trained Italian infantrymen.

black market Illegal trading in scarce or rationed goods.

bourgeois Middle class.

bureaucracy Government by officials.

capitalist One who derives his income from private ownership of industry, trade, banking or the ownership of land.

closed shop Access to employment depends on membership of a trade union.

constitution Laws on which the government of a country is based.

coup (*coup d'etat*) An attempt to overthrow the government by violent means.

deflation A situation in which there is less money available relative to its buying power.

encyclical A letter sent by the Pope to all his bishops.

ex cathedra Spoken with the authority of the Pope.

extensive farming When previously unused land is brought into cultivation.

franchise The right to vote.

Führer Leader – title taken by Hitler in Nazi Germany.

gold standard   The currency of a country has a value based on gold.

hierarchy   A group of people in control.

Il Duce   Leader – title taken by Mussolini in Fascist Italy.

indemnity   Compensation for loss or damage done.

inflation   An increase in the quantity of money available in relation to its buying power.

intensive farming   A situation in which the same land is repeatedly used to increase the yield.

laissez-faire   The view that State interference in industry and commerce should be kept to a minimum.

left-wing   Having radical or socialist views.

martial law   The exercise of supreme or overall power by the military.

mobilization   Preparation for war.

patronage   Support provided usually in the form of money or promotion.

protectorate   Rights of control exercised by one country over another.

putsch   Attempted seizure of power by revolution.

radical   A person who favours thorough-going reform.

ras   An Abyssinian prince; in Fascist Italy, a local leader.

real wages   The value of wages in terms of what it will actually buy.

recession   A period of decline in business and trade.

referendum   Submitting a question to the vote of the entire electorate.

right-wing   Having conservative views and opposed to socialism.

rule by decree   The right to pass laws without submitting them to a vote in parliament.

set-piece battles   Battles fought according to a prescribed plan.

sovereignty   Supreme and independent power.

sphere of influence   An area in which one nation is accepted as having the dominating interest.

squadristi   Gangs of thugs used by the Fascists to intimidate the opposition.

syndicalists   Left-wing extremists intent on overthrowing the capitalist system.

tariffs   Duties imposed on imported goods.

totalitarian   A form of government that controls every aspect of its citizens' lives.

taking it further

Suggestions for further reading

A History of Contemporary Italy 1943–1988, P. A. Ginsborg (Penguin Books, 1990)

Christ Stopped at Emboli, C. Levi (Four Square Books, 1946)

Economic History of Italy 1860–1990, V. Zamagni (OUP, 1993)

Fascism, ed. R. Griffin (OUP, 1995)

Fascism, A History, R. Eatwell (Chatto & Windus, 1995)

Fascist Italy and Nazi Germany, R. Bessel (CUP, 1996)

History of Fascism 1914–45, S. Payne (UCL, 1995)

History of the Italian People, G. Proacci (Pelican Books, 1973)

Hitler's Pope – The Secret History of Pope Pius XII, J. Cornwell (Penguin Books, 1999)

Italian Fascism, 1919–1945, P. Morgan (Macmillan, 1995)

Lime, Lemon and Sarsaparilla – the Italian Community in South Wales 1881–1945, Colin Hughes (Seren Books, 1991)

Modern Italy, M. Clark (Longman, 1984)

Mussolini and Fascist Italy, M. Blinkhorn (Methuen, 1984)

Mussolini, R. J. B. Bosworth (Hodder Headline, 2002)

Mussolini, J. Ridley (Constable, 1997)

Mussolini and Fascism, M. Palla (Interlink Books, 2000)

Mussolini and the British, R. Lamb (John Murray, 1997)

Mussolini from Socialist to Fascist, D. Williamson (Hodder & Stoughton, 1997)

Mussolini's Italy, M. Gallo (Macmillan, 1974)

Mussolini Unleashed, M. Knox (CUP, 1982)

Mussolini, D. Mack Smith (Weidenfeld & Nicholson, 1981)

Mussolini and the Rise of Italian Fascism, RNL Absalom (Methuen, 1969)

Mussolini's Roman Empire, D. Mack Smith (Penguin, 1977)

My Autobiography, B. Mussolini (The Mayfield Press, 1928)

State Control in Fascist Italy, D. Thompson (Manchester University Press, 1972)

The Fascist Experience of Italy, J. Pollard (Routledge, 1998)

The Last Days of Mussolini (After the Battle series, number 7, 1975)

Women Under Italian Fascism, A. De Grand (The Historical Journal XIX, 1976)

Years of Liberalism and Fascism, D. Evans (Hodder & Stoughton, 2003)

index